Last Call for Freedom

While Black Lives and All American Lives Still Matter

Nick Noel

.

Write Man Communications

P.O. Box 18036

Cincinnati, OH 45218

www.LastCallforFreedom.com

ISBN: 978-0-578-11467-5

Contents

Introduction

The Land of Freedom

Americans will tell you that we live in a free country. Many apparently believe that our freedom can never be taken away.

Repression Elsewhere

The people of North Korea are among the least free in the world.[i] They are poor, and many are hungry.[ii] Millions have died in famines, but propaganda and suppression of information make many believe they are better off than everyone else.

When the people of Communist China occupied Tiananmen Square for freedom of speech and the press, they were forcibly removed. Many were killed and thousands more were injured.

Rights to freedom of speech, the press, religion, self-defense, and many other rights must be suppressed to maintain control under communist and socialist regimes, and theocracies.

Repression and Propaganda in the Land of Freedom

In America, our freedom of speech and the press have been gradually diminished, while we have been conditioned, often by subtle means, to ignore the loss of our rights and freedom.

Words that seem similar are used to mislead us in media and education. School children are taught that the US Constitution is "a set of principles," instead of the founding law that created our federal government and on which all federal authority is based.

Mass media drowns out serious discussion of issues under a flood of propaganda and misinformation, and suppresses much information that government leaders don't like.

Political speech has been reduced to personal insults, and we have been conditioned to regard valid criticism of government policies as just bickering over details.

.

Many Americans are now repulsed by attempts to discuss our freedom and the protection of our rights, when discussion of our principles is urgently needed, and attacks on our freedom, prosperity, and security are increasing.

We have been lulled by a long period of peace and security within our borders. But while our attention has been on sports, movies, shopping, TV, and other diversions that free people have the time to enjoy, a socialist revolution has been destroying the foundation of our country and its ability to protect our freedom.

Our government doesn't censor our news or directly control its content yet. The dominant political party controls most of it.

They have caused the racial inequality in our country, but they use their control over the media to blame others, and to encourage violence, hatred, and destruction of property in response to the injustices they have caused.

They allow others to commit violence against Americans to help them destroy our rights. After a Muslim terrorist killed 49 Americans in Orlando, our leaders used mass media to blame the slaughter on our freedom of religion and right to self-defense.

Few notice the dominant political party's use of government force to punish freedom of speech, even as they now prepare to file criminal charges against people who disagree with them. [iii]

They disguise their fight against our rights in many ways to persuade good people to support their policies with good intentions, while they divide us to destroy our freedom.

My purpose is not to offend the people who have supported them with good intentions, but we can't give them four more years to destroy our freedom.

If you are offended, I hope you overcome your reluctance to discuss and defend our freedom now, before it condemns all of us and our children and grandchildren to living like the people of North Korea, Communist China, or many other countries where people can only wish they had rights and freedom to protect.

1

American Freedom vs. Subjugation

The Land of Freedom and Prosperity

Americans live in a land of freedom, security, peace, and prosperity today because the United States was founded on the principle that all people possess natural rights granted by God, and because of the limited government our founders designed and built to protect our freedom.

The Rewards of Freedom

The "Blessings of Liberty," as our founders called them,[iv] are made possible by the protection of our natural rights.

Inventions have flowed from the US. American light bulbs, telephones, automobiles, TVs, airplanes, computers, and internet have improved the standard of living here and around the world.

Freedom has made us prosperous. Even poor Americans generally have clean drinking water, food, clothing, and live in heated buildings. Many have cars, cell phones, and cable TV.

Education is available to all, although some of it is not of good quality. We have free access to computers, newspapers and books at public libraries. Any American can improve his or her condition in life through hard work and education.

There are no permanent classes here. Freedom and free enterprise, called capitalism, have enabled millions of Americans to become successful and wealthy through their skills and labor.

Many who started with little have made fortunes in business, sports and entertainment, or achieved success in other ways.

Clarence Thomas, whose ancestors were slaves, rose to become one of our most important defenders of freedom for all Americans as a US Supreme Court Justice.

Condoleezza Rice overcame living amid racial violence in which her friend and three other girls were murdered, to become

3

a college professor and provost, and to protect our freedom as US National Security Advisor and US Secretary of State.

Ben Carson used his intelligence and skills to save lives as a brain surgeon and serve as Director of Pediatric Neurosurgery at a leading research and teaching hospital.

But Today, Our Country and Our Freedom are Collapsing

The government our founders built to protect us and our freedom has been fundamentally transformed to serve a different purpose. The limits that protected our freedom have been progressively destroyed, leading some Americans to argue whether "Black lives matter" or "All lives matter."

Our country and our freedom are collapsing today because those who oppose our founding principles of equal freedom and natural rights are winning their relentless fight to destroy the limited government built to protect our freedom.

Subjugation vs. Freedom

The fight over rights began here in the colonies, before our founders were born. The king claimed a divine right to rule over the colonists, and encouraged them to subjugate African slaves.

Some of his subjects claimed they had a right to rule over their black slaves, whom they considered inferior to them.

But our leading founders wrote that all men are endowed by God with equal rights, including life, liberty, and the pursuit of happiness. They meant all humans.

Thomas Jefferson, the primary author of the Declaration of Independence, called slavery a "cruel war against human nature itself, violating its most sacred rights of life and liberty." [v]

The US Constitution: Protection of Freedom

When people truly live together in freedom, each person's freedom must be limited by the right of others to be free, but no more than necessary for that purpose.

Our founders built a government to protect our freedom through a strong national defense and the rule of law. They limited its powers to protect citizens from the government.

4

The Constitution did not create a democracy, but a republic under which individual rights can't be voted away by a majority. It didn't grant government powers to solve all our problems, but to protect our freedom and ability to solve our own problems.

Slavery: The Flaw in Our Foundation

The flaw in the US Constitution was that it didn't abolish slavery. Our leading founders, including slave owners, proposed setting a date to abolish slavery, but they were blocked by others.

They needed to establish a government to ensure national defense, so the leaders compromised, temporarily, they thought.

The Constitution discouraged slavery and allowed Congress to ban the slave trade after twenty years, but didn't end slavery. Their Northwest Ordinance prohibited the spread of slavery.

The Organized Force Against Freedom

Slavery led to the rise of an enduring force against freedom when the modern Democratic Party (first called Jacksonians) was founded in the 1820s by slave owners to protect slavery and promote more equality among white men.

Their fight to protect slavery was not a disagreement over a political issue, but directly opposed our founding principle that all people possess God-given natural rights.

Slave owners claimed that God made the black race unfit for anything except slavery, and gave slave owners a right to use them, as well as a duty to feed, clothe, house, and control them.

In the Dred Scott case, the Democratic Supreme Court Chief Justice wrote that inferiority of the black race was well-known. He ruled that a black man could never be a citizen even if freed from slavery, because a citizen has a right to speak freely and the right to own a gun, making him a truly free man.

Democrats didn't respect the rights of Native American Indians, either. In violation of valid treaties, they forced the "civilized tribes" off their lands, and into the "Trail of Tears" death marches that killed many thousands as they were driven to reservations west of the Mississippi River.

Slavery to Segregation

Democrats lost their ability to enslave black people in 1865, a few years after the Republican Party was founded to oppose slavery in 1854. Republicans abolished slavery and established citizenship and voting rights for the former slaves through the 13th, 14th, and 15th Amendments after the Civil War.

But Democrats quickly regained power, to subjugate black people through segregation, Ku Klux Klan (KKK) terrorism, and gun control laws to keep black men from defending themselves.

Progressives, Socialists, and Segregationist Democrats

In the early 1900s, Democrats aligned with the progressive movement, which rejected the principle of natural rights, and claimed human rights should be determined by government. vi

Progressives and compromisers among the Republican Party helped them destroy important Constitutional limits through the 16th Amendment income tax and creation of the Federal Reserve.

Then, socialist union bosses who favored keeping black men from being able to compete with white union workers joined forces with the segregationist Democrats.

Combining Socialism with Segregation

We've been led to believe the Great Depression was caused by a failure of free enterprise and a lack of government control, and was finally ended by President Franklin D. Roosevelt (FDR) and his New Deal programs. But that story is untrue.

Republicans helped cause it. But when Democrats took complete control, their New Deal prolonged the Depression into ten years of misery and fear for Americans. They ignored the Constitution, destroyed its limits, and began transforming our government to follow steps from the Communist Manifesto.

Those steps include taxes that punish high incomes, abolition of property rights, confiscation of property, central control over credit, banking, communications, transportation, factories, and farm lands, and indoctrination of all children in public schools from the earliest possible age. And effectively, one more that Marx and Engels predicted in 1848:

"...In America, where a democratic constitution has already been established, the communists must make the common cause with the party which will turn this constitution against the bourgeoisie (the middle class)..." [vii]

World War II ended the Depression. Segregation continued.

The Struggle for Equal Rights

Segregation and racial discrimination were rampant and accepted. The KKK, the unofficial enforcement arm of the Democratic Party, terrorized black Americans with impunity.

Civil rights organizations began winning victories for equal rights in the 1950s and early 60s. Two important leaders were Malcolm X and Reverend Dr. Martin Luther King, Jr. (MLK).

Individual black men broke down walls of segregation with their superior skills in sports and entertainment.

Republican Dwight Eisenhower became the first president in 80 years to use federal power to enforce equal rights for black people, and he implemented desegregation of US Armed Forces.

Eisenhower also proposed and signed the first two federal civil rights laws enacted since Reconstruction, in 1957 and 1960.

Senator Lyndon B. Johnson (LBJ) led Democrat opposition to the civil rights laws. But when he lost his party's presidential nomination, he suddenly pretended to support equal civil rights.

John F. Kennedy (JFK), who had been a junior senator under Johnson, was elected president. Upon JFK's 1963 assassination, LBJ was there as vice president to instantly replace him.

The Dream vs. the Reality

During the struggle to overcome segregation in 1963, MLK told us of his dream about freedom, justice, and equal rights. [viii] It was much like earlier dreams of Frederick Douglass, who was born a slave and later used his abilities to help abolish slavery.

King dreamed of a day when black and white Americans would share our freedom equally, and judge each other, not by the color of our skin, but by the content of our character. Democrats have stopped MLK's dream from coming true.

Transformation to Socialist Control Over All Americans

LBJ signed, then defeated the purpose of the Civil Rights Act of 1964 with socialist programs that gave Democrats more control over black people than they had exercised since slavery.

Instead of enforcing the civil rights laws Republicans had worked for a century to pass, he substituted socialist programs to make civil rights leaders believe Democrats had changed.

Malcolm X wasn't fooled. He spoke up to expose LBJ's lies to black Americans, but he was assassinated a few days later.

Mass Media Propaganda (MMP) effectively replaced the KKK as the Democratic Party's enforcement arm, and began consistently blaming racial discrimination on Republicans who refused to accept socialist programs as a substitute for equality.

Now, instead of living as equals 50 years later, millions of black Americans who failed to escape, live segregated amid crime and violence on Democrat-controlled urban plantations.

The education of black children in many public schools is so poor that black educator Walter Williams calls it "fraudulent." [ix]

The time is long overdue for us to recognize that Democrats are still the party of slavery. The core values of their leaders are still that they have a right to control other people, and that black people are inferior to whites, which they try to disguise today.

They have expanded their goal from enslaving black people to controlling all of us, and evolved to lead a progressive fight against the principles of freedom and limited government.

Supreme Court's Destruction of Freedom

The Supreme Court's duty is to apply the law correctly, not to write laws or change them for the supposed general welfare. It is not a political body intended to be balanced. Our freedom and natural rights are not political issues, except to Democrats.

But the US Supreme Court defies the Constitution. Only three of nine Justices have performed their duty in recent years, and one of them has died. Two are rogues, and four consistently rule against our freedom. If US senators disregard their duty and approve one more socialist, the Court majority will stand against the Constitution, and we will probably never regain our freedom.

Limits Broken; Government Turned Against Its Purpose

Democrats have turned our federal government against its purpose of protecting us and our freedom. They've broken the limits protecting us, with help from compromising Republicans and absurd Supreme Court rulings. Here's how it's working out:

Promises vs. Reality

Millions of seniors are hooked on a bankrupt Social Security System with no money and no legal obligation to pay benefits. Every payment depends on tax collections and borrowing.

US national debt is $19 trillion, or $60,000 for each of us. With many times that in future liabilities, our leaders are stealing from our grandchildren by borrowing even more in their name.

Millions of Americans are hooked on welfare and food stamps, while poverty rates remain substantially unchanged.

Businesses are hooked on government subsidies and favors that distort free enterprise and create "crony capitalism."

Mass Media Propaganda and educational indoctrination control us. Democrats use them to encourage racial violence over injustices they have created, and wage a war against police.

If you think that the issues of slavery, segregation, and equal rights affect only black people, you are sadly and dangerously mistaken. They affect all Americans, and always have.

We are on the brink of losing all our freedom to a collapse worse than the Great Depression, war in our streets, or both.

Democrats are dismantling our national defense, allowing aliens to attack us within our borders, and enabling Muslim terrorists to obtain nuclear weapons to kill us and our allies.

We Can Still Choose Freedom, if We Do It Now

We can probably still survive as a land of freedom where all lives matter without a violent new revolution if we take action now. If we don't do it now, we will lose that ability.

This is not about just changing your political party. We need to remove the force against freedom from power, demand equal protection, and stop treating human rights as political issues.

If we don't use our votes now to remove the party of slavery, segregation, and socialism from power and preserve the freedom we were given, we may never have another chance to get it back.

What We Must Do to Save Our Freedom

We need American men and women of all ages and races to understand our principles of freedom, how our founders secured our rights, and how our natural rights are being extinguished.

We have been conditioned by more than 50 years of MMP, school indoctrination, and suppression of information, to reject the truth about Democrats as a political difference of opinion.

But we need to overcome the myths, distortions, and lies about our country, our freedom, and our history that have been drummed into us. And we must choose freedom.

Thomas Paine wrote in *Common Sense*, "…a long habit of not thinking a thing wrong, gives it a superficial appearance of being right…" [x]

KCarl Smith, founder of the Frederick Douglass Republicans wrote, "My lack of knowing the true history of both parties (Republican and Democratic) twisted my whole outlook on politics. As a result, others easily persuaded me." [xi]

We need to break the habit of accepting propaganda and indoctrination in government-controlled schools as right.

The time is short, and we need to act now. My attempt to inform and alert my fellow Americans is on the following pages.

You can pass this book on to others, check out the many references cited, and discuss our freedom with others now.

Reverend King told us 53 years ago, "Now is the time!"

But this may be our last chance. Today, the time to preserve our freedom is probably now or never.

10

2

Freedom in the American Colonies

Beavers, Monkeys, Kings, and Men

Freedom, more than intelligence, is the defining difference between humans and other animals on earth. Wild animals are said to be free, but their freedom isn't the same as ours. The clearest distinction between humans and other animals is that we can to choose whether or not to follow our natural instincts.

Other animals can perform complicated tasks. Beavers cut down trees to build dams and dwellings, and even choose the right locations to build them. Monkeys are capable of using tools to accomplish certain tasks. They possess intelligence, but not the freedom to make the kinds of choices humans can make.

But despite our free will, men have historically been ruled by kings, queens, emperors, czars, pharaohs, and other rulers who have often claimed a divine right to rule, which has been passed down from one generation of their family to the next.

Some royal families have held power for many years, fighting and even killing each other to determine their order of succession, while ceremonial rituals and extravagant trappings of power intimidate subjects into accepting their legitimacy.

Thomas Paine, one of our founders, blasted claims of divine right in *Common Sense*, describing how the Norman Conquest of 1066 established the line of monarchs who ruled England. He wrote that the first king in any line of succession was likely…

"…nothing better than the principal ruffian of some restless gang, whose savage manners… obtained him the title of chief among plunderers…"

Paine described William the Conqueror, their first king, as…

"…landing with an armed banditti, and establishing himself king of England against the consent of the natives…" [xii]

11

Government is necessary to maintain freedom, but it has often been the enemy of freedom. Kings and other elite rulers use it to impose their will on others, and maintain their power by using it to grant favors to supporters and punish opponents.

Royals and religious despots, sometimes the same people, and often in collusion with each other, have historically punished challengers in evil and dehumanizing ways.

During colonial days, rule by monarchs was well-accepted in England, Europe, and elsewhere. Living as subjects was not unusual, but the American colonists were unusual subjects.

Many thousands of them made individual decisions in the 1600s and 1700s to risk their lives and all their possessions, sail across the Atlantic Ocean, and establish new lives here.

The journey was long and risky. It took 66 days for the 102 pilgrims and their crew of sailors aboard the Mayflower in 1620. Two died on the way, and almost half of the rest perished during their first winter here. Hardship and death were accepted risks.

The colonists were motivated by their religious convictions, thirst for freedom, and hope for opportunity, while their friends and relatives chose to remain safely behind.

British monarchs wanted the American colonies to grow, to expand their power and wealth. So they granted charters that allowed colonists a freedom they didn't have in England or in most of Europe--to openly practice their own religious beliefs.

The colonists didn't all share the same religious beliefs, but many were Christians. Some held such strong convictions that they brought their families here primarily for religious freedom.

The colonies grew and thrived. In 1770, the total population of the English colonies in America exceeded 2 million people.

Colonists built cities, established local governments, and elected their own local officials. The British Army provided defense, but its purpose was to protect the interests of the king.

As the British crown changed hands, some monarchs granted more freedom, and others less.

3

The American Revolution

Original Tea Party Extremists Who Refused to Compromise

After the colonists had governed themselves to a great extent for many years, the king and Parliament raised taxes and tried to tighten their control. Colonists reacted by openly questioning the legitimacy of the king's rule.

Samuel Adams of Massachusetts led resistance to taxation without representation, and organized communications among patriots from all 13 colonies. John Hancock used his wealth to support the colonial cause and was a leader in the Continental Congress. John Adams, later second US President, championed the right to counsel and opposition to the Stamp Act of 1765.

Benjamin Franklin of Pennsylvania promoted the rights of citizens, unified colonists in the cause of independence, and traveled to England and France to represent the colonies.

Patrick Henry gave impassioned speeches urging independence in the Virginia Convention, at which Thomas Jefferson and George Washington were also delegates. George Mason wrote the Virginia Declaration of Rights.

Most of these leaders and over three hundred others from the thirteen colonies participated at times in the First and Second Continental Congress as representatives of their colonies.

Words of defiance and acts of resistance led to clashes in the Liberty Affair of 1768, the Boston Massacre of 1770, and the Boston Tea Party of 1773, as colonists opposed the king's new taxes and his efforts to strengthen his control.

The struggle escalated into military confrontations beginning in 1775. The American Revolution began in Massachusetts with the battles of Lexington and Concord in April 1775, as Paul Revere made his famous ride to warn members of the colonial militia that British troops were coming to take their weapons.

By the time the colonists formally declared their independence, the fighting had already been underway for more than a year.

The Continental Congress then produced a document, written by Thomas Jefferson and others, setting forth their intentions and the reasons for their actions. On July 4, 1776, the Congress approved the Declaration of Independence, and members finished signing the final copy on August 2.

Their Declaration boldly stated that individual men, not kings, possess natural rights granted by God.

"...We hold these truths to be self-evident, that all men are created equal, that they are endowed by their Creator with certain unalienable Rights, that among these are Life, Liberty and the pursuit of Happiness.--"

"...--That to secure these rights, Governments are instituted among Men, deriving their just powers from the consent of the governed, — That whenever any Form of Government becomes destructive of these ends, it is the Right of the People to alter or to abolish it, and to institute new Government..." [xiii]

Thomas Jefferson

Americans Risked Everything for Freedom, and Almost Lost

By declaring independence, our founders risked their lives and everything they had. Torture and execution had been traditional punishments for treason against the king, and their

Declaration could certainly be considered treasonous. But by that time, not being free had become unacceptable to them.

Americans were fighting a war that would take many lives and destroy much of their property. There was so much at stake that they had to prevail, but they almost lost the war during the first six months after their Declaration of Independence.

Commanding General George Washington's troops were severely defeated in the Battle of Long Island in August 1776. Nathan Hale was hanged by the British in September. The navy was mostly destroyed on Lake Champlain in October. The army was defeated at White Plains and Manhattan, New York, and Fort Lee, New Jersey. The Newport, Rhode Island naval base was captured by the British in December, all before the army won two critical victories at Trenton and Princeton, New Jersey.

Come from Behind Victory for Freedom

An observer described being able to follow a trail of blood left by Washington's troops as they marched through snow on their way to winning a surprise victory at Trenton on December 26, 1776. They quickly stunned the British again, defeating them at Princeton in early January. These two victories kept the American fight for freedom alive, but the war was far from over.

American troops gained ground in many battles to drive the British out of strategic areas, but also suffered devastating defeats that threatened their cause.

The war was made more difficult by the many loyalists who supported the king living throughout the colonies. There were friends, neighbors, and relatives of US leaders and soldiers who wanted the revolution to fail.

Families of patriots risked their safety and made sacrifices to help them. Abigail Adams hid soldiers in her home and made bullets for them from her metal household items.

The relatively untrained and unprepared Americans persevered for seven long years. They eventually received help from France and support from Spain, while paid Hessian troops and some American Indian warriors aided the British troops.

George Washington
Portrait by Rembrandt Steele

The conditions under which American troops fought were often horrible, and sometimes worse. Approximately 25,000 Americans died fighting the war, about two-thirds from sickness and disease. The same percentage of the U.S. population today would be about 2 million people.

In the final decisive battle, Americans won a major victory at Yorktown, Virginia in October 1781. After a few more battles in 1782, the British withdrew. The Treaty of Paris, officially ending the war, was signed in September, 1783.

Historians often ignore the many black American patriots who contributed to the war from start to finish. Among them, Peter Salem was known as a hero of Bunker Hill, and James Armistead was known for helping win battles including the last major one at Yorktown through his spying against the British.

Unlike rebels in other countries, Americans weren't led by a charismatic leader who wanted to become the next king. Washington and other American leaders didn't want to be kings. They fought because they wanted to live together in freedom.

Americans won their independence after a long, hard war, but their next challenge was to maintain their freedom.

After the Revolution: New Issues

The Revolution would have been pointless if Americans couldn't live together in freedom, so they had to face new issues.

They had to be prepared to defend themselves again if necessary. They wanted to promote commerce between States, and needed a way to settle disputes to keep their freedom from being destroyed by conflicts between States. Also, not everyone in America was free.

Living Together in Freedom: What it Means

When people truly live together in freedom, each person's freedom must be limited by the right of others to be free, but no more than necessary for that purpose. People living together in freedom are not restricted in their pursuit of happiness as long as they honor the equal right of others to be free.

"...--That to secure these rights, Governments are instituted among Men, deriving their just powers from the consent of the governed" [xiv]

Americans needed to institute a new government.

Preparing to Defend Freedom Together

The British army and navy were still powerful forces, and British troops remained along the northern border in Canada. The king could attempt to re-conquer his former colonies, or other countries might try to conquer them.

The thirteen colonies were now States, or independent countries. They had depleted many resources and lost many lives fighting the long war. Some of their soldiers had not received promised pay, and other war debts remained unpaid.

The States were said to be united, but their Continental Congress didn't have any taxing authority to raise the funds necessary to pay off their war debts or prepare for the future.

Keeping the States united and able to defend against any new threat might have been impossible without paying off their debts.

A united effort had been required to win independence, and it was unlikely that any State or lesser group of States could withstand an attack by Great Britain or another world power. A strong, united military effort would almost certainly be necessary at some point to defend their newly won freedom.

Maintaining Peace Among Free States

Under the king's rule, commercial activity had flowed freely across colonial borders, but differences between independent States could lead to wars between them.

Some States might charge higher taxes or impose business regulations on individuals from other States that would limit free trade across their borders. The occasional skirmishes arising between citizens of different States could escalate into wars.

Lack of uniform currency and rules of commerce could also become serious problems in conducting business between people of different States. Conflicts over transportation across State lines, the building of bridges and roadways, access to ports, and navigation of interstate waterways all threatened to disrupt unity.

Americans needed to resolve these problems to preserve freedom, but they didn't want to create a central government that could usurp the powers of their State governments and threaten the rights of citizens. A powerful central government could become as oppressive as the king and Parliament, or worse.

Not Everyone Was Free

The other problem the former colonists faced in preserving freedom was that not everyone among them was free. Roughly 17 percent of the people who lived in the States were slaves.

In a country where a war for freedom had just been won, slavery had survived. A minority of Americans, including some of our founders, owned many slaves. But most Americans didn't own slaves, and many wanted to abolish slavery.

Slavery was a divisive issue that was destined to become much more divisive.

Slavery: A Most Divisive Issue

Slavery Wasn't Born in America

Just as people have been ruled by monarchs and other absolute rulers for centuries, slavery has also been a fact of life around the world through most of history.

The Egyptians enslaved the Israelites. Ancient Greeks and Romans enslaved the people of conquered lands. Slavery existed in Europe, mostly evolving into serfdom during the middle ages. Irish Catholics who survived genocide under English rule in the 1600s were forced into slavery. Slavery has a long history in China and other Far East countries, where it continues today.

Native American tribes took members of defeated tribes as slaves before Europeans arrived here, and European explorers began using natives as slaves soon after Columbus discovered America in 1492. African tribes have practiced genocide for centuries, keeping some defeated tribe members as slaves, and the practice continues today. In fact, many African slaves in America had been sold to slave traders by other African tribes.

Slavery of black Africans here began in the early 1600s, and grew during colonial days, especially in the southern colonies, where huge plantations with many slaves produced cash crops.

Plantation owners were the rulers within their plantations, building work forces and their own societies. Slaves performed various jobs, but most worked as laborers in the fields. Some worked as slave bosses, directing the work of others, and some lived as subservient members of their owners' households.

Slaves were treated as property. They were generally slaves for life, with little or no hope of ever becoming free. Children born into slavery became slaves for life.

African slaves in America were just as human as the slave owners, but they were humans of a different race who had been taken from foreign lands and subjugated. That didn't make them less human, but made it more convenient for slave owners and many others to regard them as inferior, or less human.

The Difference between a Subject and a Slave

There were parallels, but also stark differences between living as subjects of a king, and living as slaves.

Through taxes and regulations, the king infringed upon the natural rights of his subjects. He effectively owned part of what their labor produced and controlled some aspects of their lives. But since he didn't actually own his subjects, he didn't provide for their individual needs.

The slave owner completely denied the natural rights of his slaves. He owned everything their labor produced and controlled every aspect of their lives. Because he even owned their bodies, he provided whatever food, shelter, clothing, education, training, and medical care he deemed necessary for them, such as it was.

Some slave owners considered themselves great benefactors to the primitive black slaves for whom they provided benefits.

British rule had been more overbearing than Americans were willing to tolerate, but their lives as subjects were starkly superior to the lives of slaves whose owners provided for them.

Our Founders Who Owned Slaves Tried to Abolish Slavery

Slavery was a fact of life in the colonies. Our founders, including many who owned slaves, recognized that slavery was wrong, and knew it couldn't be allowed to continue forever.

Most Americans recognized the moral problem with continuing to allow some men among them to be so thoroughly deprived of their freedom as slaves, and many wanted to abolish slavery immediately.

Disagreement over slavery threatened to derail proposed solutions to the first three problems our founders faced, and struck at the heart of their own struggle for freedom.

6

Surprising Facts About the US Constitution

Our Freedom Wouldn't Be Worth Much Without It

Ask any American what has made the United States a great country, and one of the answers you're likely get is "freedom." But freedom isn't worth much if it can be taken away by foreign invaders, by your neighbors, or by your own government.

Foundation of the Structure That Protects Our Freedom

The government structure our founding fathers designed and built to protect our freedom is what has made it possible for Americans to build the United States into the great country it is today. They created that structure through the US Constitution.

They stated their principles of freedom and government in the Declaration of Independence, and built a government based on those principles through the US Constitution.

How The Constitution Was Designed

The Articles of Confederation that held the colonies together during the war weren't adequate to permanently maintain freedom after the colonies became independent States.

After years of discussing how to amend the Articles of Confederation, our founders instead created a completely new form of government. During one summer of intense debate, prayer, and problem-solving in 1787, they designed a new government to permanently protect the freedom of US citizens.

George Washington, commanding general of the US Army during the Revolution and later first US president, was president of the Constitutional Convention. James Madison, who later served as fourth US president, was one of the principal authors.

Leaders from twelve of the thirteen States participated. Ratification by at least nine states was required. Eleven States ratified it by the end of 1788, and the other two by 1790.

Worthless Without Limits

Americans needed to create a strong union to protect their freedom, but if they gave a new government too much power, its leaders could become as oppressive as the king and Parliament, or worse. They purposely didn't grant their government powers to solve all their problems, but only to protect their freedom.

As the States debated ratification, principal author James Madison wrote in the Federalist Papers, Number 45,

"...The powers delegated by the proposed Constitution to the Federal Government, are few and defined. Those which are to remain in the State Governments are numerous and indefinite. The former will be exercised principally on external objects, as war, peace, negotiation, and foreign commerce; with which last the power of taxation will, for the most part, be connected.

The powers reserved to the several States will extend to all the objects which, in the ordinary course of affairs, concern the lives, liberties, and properties of the people, and the internal order, improvement, and prosperity of the State. The operations of the federal government will be most extensive and important in times of war and danger; those of the State governments, in times of peace and security..." [xv]

Not Written to Grant Rights to Citizens

Before the US Constitution, government documents about rights of the people generally defined and limited specific rights that the king or other government was willing to grant them. But the granting in our Constitution flowed in the opposite direction.

Our founders wrote in the Declaration of Independence that all men are born with natural rights, that legitimate governments are instituted among men to secure their rights, and that they derive their just powers from the consent of the governed.

An important thing to understand about the US Constitution is that it was not written to grant rights to individual citizens or define our rights. The rights of citizens were not even addressed except to specifically uphold a few traditional rights, mostly of defendants under prosecution.

The Constitution was written to define and limit the specific powers that the people and the States were willing to grant to the new federal government they were instituting to secure their rights. Any power they did not grant through the Constitution does not lawfully belong to the federal government.

The US Government is Not a Democracy

Our government is not a democracy. The founders had no intention of creating one, and the word isn't even mentioned in the Constitution. A democracy can satisfy the immediate will of the majority, while failing to protect the rights of the minority.

Democracy alone can't secure freedom. In many cases, all it does is allow people to help pick the next tyrant who will rule over them. The people get to choose what most of them want at the moment, but without limits to protect their rights, democracy can empower an evil dictator such as a Stalin or a Hitler.

The US government is a republican form of government. Most of our leaders are chosen through democratic elections, but their powers are limited by the Constitution, and natural rights of individuals can't be voted away by a majority of the voters.

Our government is described as a government of laws, not of men, because our freedom is protected by the rule of law, not legitimately subject to the whims of powerful men.

The Constitution Specifies a Process for Making Changes

Our founders realized that the people might want to make changes. But because Constitutional limits on federal power are so essential to preserving freedom, the Constitution requires consent by two thirds of Congress and three fourths of the States for Amendments. No approval by the president is required. After ratification, the same process is required to change them.

The US Constitution Does Not Require Interpretation

The US Constitution is written in English, and the limited powers that the people and States granted to the federal government are clearly stated. They are not written in a foreign language or a secret code that can be understood only by Supreme Court justices.

They are not legitimately subject to interpretation according to the laws of any foreign country, the teachings of any religion, new meanings of words, or opinion polls.

Nothing allows unconstitutional actions by the president, Congress, or the Supreme Court to supersede the Constitution.

The Constitution grants the Supreme Court power to apply the Constitution and other laws correctly, and to judge whether lower courts have applied them correctly. It does not grant the Court any authority to "interpret" or change laws, or "legislate from the bench."

Further, the Constitution does not grant the Supreme Court authority to effectively substitute its own previous rulings for the words of the Constitution.

The Constitution is the sole basis for the Supreme Court's authority, so for the Court to regard its own prior rulings as of higher authority than the Constitution because the issue was previously decided defies logic. Judicial precedent that differs from the Constitution is not a lawful basis for any court decision.

The Constitution Did Not Declare Each Slave to be Three Fifths of a Person

This purposeful lie about the Constitution has been repeated many times, but it's still a lie. Anyone who says the original words of the Constitution declared each slave to be only three-fifths of a person is either ignorant or lying.

The three-fifths compromise was only about voting power and taxes, and was made to limit the ability of slave owners to perpetuate slavery.

The numbers of Representatives and presidential electors for each State, and apportionment of any direct federal taxes to be levied against each State, were to be determined by population.

States with many slaves wanted to count all of them in their population figures to gain federal voting power, but didn't want to count them for the apportionment of taxes.

Opponents of slavery argued that slave owners should not be allowed to inflate their voting power by counting people who were not free to vote. They didn't want any slaves to be counted. The compromise discouraged slavery by allowing only three-fifths of the number of slaves to be used in those calculations for as long as slavery continued to exist in those States.

The compromise has no effect today, because all references to slavery were effectively replaced and superseded by the 13th, 14th, and 15th Amendments in 1865, 1868, and 1870.

The Constitution Set a Date for Banning the Slave Trade

Many Americans, including our founders who owned slaves, wanted to abolish slavery through the Constitution. Thomas Jefferson began proposing in 1784 that slavery be abolished after 1800, but his proposals were defeated. George Washington freed his slaves upon his death in 1799.

Our founders needed a ratified Constitution to ensure national defense and domestic tranquility. They weren't able to achieve ratification and abolish slavery at the same time. So they allowed the States 20 years to end slavery on their own terms, barring Congress from banning the slave trade until 1808.

The Flaw In the US Constitution

It was widely believed that Congress would ban the slave trade at the first opportunity, and slavery would end soon after. The first part was correct. Congress banned the slave trade in1808, and Jefferson, serving as the third US president, signed the bill into law. But slavery was not abolished until 1865.

The US Constitution recognized slavery and allowed it to continue for a time that our leading founders assumed would be only temporary. This was a serious flaw that eventually required a devastating war and three constitutional amendments to repair.

A country of free men with laws based on the natural rights of men could not allow slavery, the opposite of freedom, to continue indefinitely. Slavery was allowed to exist far too long. Although they were treated as property, the slaves were people whose natural rights were wrongfully violated.

7

Our Foundation: Limited Powers Granted

From the People and States To the Federal Government

Through the US Constitution, the people and States granted powers to the federal government they were creating. It is important to understand these powers, because no other federal powers legitimately exist, except any granted by Amendments.

A short summary is below. A summary with more details and a full list of all Amendments to the US Constitution are in the appendix following the last chapter. You can easily obtain a copy of the full original text from any public library or online.

Three Separate but Unequal Branches

The Constitution specifies federal powers and duties, and divides them among three intentionally unequal branches.

Congress was obviously intended to be the most powerful. The president's main duties are to command US national defense and to approve and execute the laws passed by Congress. The Supreme Court's duty is to apply the Constitution and laws passed by Congress, not to change or modify them.

The limits and the division of powers were both important because the people were creating a new government and granting it powers that could cost Americans their freedom or their lives.

Enumerating these powers would have been completely unnecessary and superfluous if their intention had been to simply grant unlimited powers to the federal government.

Article I. (1) Creates Congress, grants Congress exclusive power to make laws and declare war, and enumerates specific federal powers. Federal laws were intended to be few, and limited to the powers granted. Congress was required to meet only once each year, in sessions expected to be short.

Places further restrictions on federal powers, including no prohibition of the slave trade until 1808, and restricts specific powers of the States that conflict with powers granted to the federal government.

The three-fifths compromise reduces federal voting power of individual States for as long as they continue to allow slavery.

Vesting all legislative powers in Congress assured the people and the States that they would not be subject to any laws not reviewed and approved by their representatives and senators.

Article II. (2) Creates the offices of president and vice president, establishes the president as the commander in chief of US military forces, to be raised and regulated by Congress,

Grants him powers, "by and with the Advice and Consent of the Senate," to make Treaties, appoint Supreme Court justices and other public officials; authorizes impeachment by Congress.

The president's duty is to execute the laws. He can suggest new laws, and he can require that a larger majority of Congress vote to enact a law if he disagrees.

Article III. (3) Creates and vests judicial power in the Supreme Court and inferior courts established by Congress.

Grants the Court judicial power over all cases arising under the Constitution, and laws made under its authority, and requires trial by jury in the State where a crime was committed.

The Supreme Court has no authority to make or change laws or set policies. Its only authority is to correctly apply the Constitution and laws of Congress.

Defines Treason and limits the punishment for Treason.

Article IV. (4) Establishes relationships between State laws and federal laws, and enumerates further powers of Congress.

.

Establishes the duty of the United States to guarantee to every State a Republican Form of Government, and protect each against invasion, and domestic violence, upon request.

Article V. (5) Establishes procedures for legitimate changes. Amendments require approval by two thirds majority of both Houses of Congress and ratification by three fourths of the States. No approval by the president is required.

Article VI. (6) Assumes national public debt, adopts this Constitution, and laws and treaties made under its authority as the supreme law of the land. Requires that all federal and State legislators, judicial and executive officers be bound by Oath or Affirmation to support the US Constitution.

Article VII. (7) Establishes ratification procedures, and requires ratification by nine States.

Ratification and The Bill of Rights

Eleven of the 13 States ratified the Constitution by the end of 1788, some of them demanding amendments to further guarantee that the new federal government would not infringe upon their rights by exceeding the limited powers they granted.

The United States government began operating in 1789. The 12th and 13th States ratified the Constitution by 1790.

Amendments demanded by the States followed shortly thereafter. Collectively known as the Bill of Rights, the first ten amendments were ratified together and added to the Constitution in 1791. The US Declaration of Independence and the US Constitution, including its Bill of Rights, are often called our country's founding documents.

A summary with more details and notes, and a full list of all Amendments to the US Constitution can be found in the appendix, following the last chapter of this book.

8

The Bill of Rights

Not Written to Grant Rights to People

The first ten amendments, known as the Bill of Rights, were not written to grant rights, but to protect the rights of the people and the States by further limiting the federal government's ability to abuse the powers they had just granted it. Several of these Amendments affirm rights already understood to belong to the people, and prohibit government from violating them.

The duties and powers of the federal government are enumerated in the US Constitution, and no other powers were granted. Some of our founders, including John Adams and Alexander Hamilton, saw that limitation as sufficient. But others were correctly concerned about the potential for abuse. George Mason, Elbridge Gerry, and Edmund Randolph refused to sign the Constitution because more specific limits were not included.

Mason, whose ideas had contributed to both the Declaration of Independence and the Constitution, was also the author of the Virginia Declaration of Rights. When several States demanded further limits on federal power upon ratifying the Constitution, Mason helped lead the way to the Bill of Rights.

Some argued that these Amendments were unnecessary and dangerous. One of the strongest arguments against adopting the Bill of Rights was that future tyrants and judges might misuse its words to wrongfully limit and define the rights of the people, pretending that these further guarantees of freedom were actually rights granted to the people by the government.

Of course, that is exactly what tyrannical Supreme Court justices, presidents, and members of Congress have done.

The First Ten Amendments

Amendment I (1) guarantees that the federal government will not establish an official state religion, such as the Church of

29

England, so that government can never force citizens to support a state religion or prohibit the free exercise of other religions.

"Congress shall make no law respecting an establishment of religion, or prohibiting the free exercise thereof..." [xvi]

It does not guarantee freedom from religion, nor freedom from being offended by another person's religion.

"...or abridging the freedom of speech, or of the press; or the right of the people peaceably to assemble, and to petition the Government for a redress of grievances."

Amendment II (2) protects the absolute right of every free man to defend himself, his freedom, and his property. "The right of the people to keep and bear arms" was well understood as a basic difference between free men and men who are not free.

"A well regulated Militia, being necessary to the security of a free State, the right of the people to keep and bear Arms, shall not be infringed."

A militia is an organization of free men for the collective self-defense of their individual rights. Our federal government is also a larger organization of free men for the self-defense of their individual rights. This Amendment is not about hunting rights.

The Second Amendment asserts maintaining a militia as just one reason why this well-understood right shall not be infringed.

Amendment III (3) guarantees that the federal government shall not infringe upon the rights of citizens by forcing them to provide food and lodging for federal troops within their own homes, except as prescribed by a specific law in time of war.

Amendment IV (4) guarantees that "the right of the people to be secure in their persons, houses, papers, and effects, against unreasonable searches and seizures, shall not be violated..." It prohibits most searches and seizures without a warrant.

Amendment V (5) guarantees that no person shall be tried for a serious crime without confirmation of probable cause by a grand jury, nor be forced to testify against himself, nor be tried again for the same crime after being found not guilty, nor be deprived of life, liberty, or property without due process of law, nor have his property taken for public use without due process.

Amendment VI (6) prohibits violating the rights of the accused. Guarantees the right to a speedy and public trial, by an impartial jury in the State and district where the crime was committed. Guarantees the accused be informed of the nature and cause of the accusation; confronted with the witnesses against him; have compulsory process for obtaining witnesses in his favor, and have the Assistance of Counsel for his defense.

Amendment VII (7) guarantees that "...the right to trial by jury shall be preserved, and no fact tried by a jury, shall be otherwise re-examined in any Court of the United States, than according to the rules of the common law."

Amendment VIII (8) limits the powers of prosecution and punishment. "Excessive bail shall not be required, nor excessive fines imposed, nor cruel and unusual punishments inflicted."

Amendment IX (9) prohibits using the words of the Constitution to justify limiting or defining rights of the people. "The enumeration in the Constitution, of certain rights, shall not be construed to deny or disparage others retained by the people."

Amendment X (10) "The powers not delegated to the United States by the Constitution, nor prohibited by it to the States, are reserved to the States respectively, or to the people."

If the limits on government powers were not important, why would they be reinforced in the Ninth and Tenth Amendments?

Neither the Constitution nor the Bill of Rights grants any power to limit the rights of the people by the tradition of English common law. But both re-enforce certain common law rights already understood to belong to free people, to guarantee that government will not infringe upon those rights.

The purpose of the Constitution was not to allow the federal government to rule by English Common Law. It is superior to English Common law in the United States, not subject to it.

All legitimate powers of the US government were granted to it through the US Constitution, and not by any other authority.

9

Life, Liberty, And the Pursuit of Happiness

Government of Laws, Not of Men

Under the Constitution, the United States is a government of laws to protect the natural rights of citizens, starting with life, liberty, and the pursuit of happiness. The last is often called the right of property, because the ability to acquire property and be secure in our enjoyment of it is a major part of happiness.

Under a government of men, by contrast, the freedom and rights of the people are subject to control by the rulers.

The Natural Right of Self Defense

Each man has a natural right to defend his life, freedom, and property, including by force. A just government, as Frederic Bastiat described it in his 1848 book, *The Law*, is the "collective organization of the individual right to lawful defense." [xvii]

It is necessary for a just government to use force to defend the lives, liberty and property of its citizens, and to punish those who wrongfully violate them. But the natural rights of the people are superior to the rights of any government.

Using government force to take property from some people and give it to others perverts the purpose of a just government.

Free People and Free Markets Create Prosperity

People exercise their rights through free exchange of goods and services with others for their goods and services by engaging in commerce. Free markets enable people to obtain better quality or lower cost by making their own choices.

As the people prospered, the United States grew rapidly, expanding into Florida, Louisiana, Texas, and all the way to the Pacific Ocean. From 1788 to 1860, 13 States grew to 33, and the population grew from 3.9 million to 31.4 million.

Slavery Prohibited in New Territories

During the first year after the US commenced operations in 1789, Congress and President George Washington enacted the Northwest Ordinance, which laid out a plan for expansion, and prohibited slavery in the territory that would become Ohio, Indiana, Illinois, Michigan, Wisconsin, and part of Minnesota.

But Freedom and Protection of Rights Not Extended to All

But as the country grew rapidly and achieved prosperity, the US government failed to protect the rights all. In violation of its treaties, the US forced Native Americans off their traditional lands in a way that caused great misery and many deaths.

And instead of fading away after enactment of the Northwest Ordinance in 1789 and prohibition of the slave trade in 1808, slavery grew and became more entrenched. Slave owners grew politically stronger and more aggressive about protecting their "right" to permanently enslave other people.

10

Parties, Slavery, and Race

The First Leaders and the Early Parties

George Washington, who didn't belong to a party, served as first US president, followed by John Adams, a Federalist.

They were followed by Thomas Jefferson, James Madison, and James Monroe, who called themselves Republicans, but are often called Democratic Republicans today. The first five were all founding fathers or had fought in the Revolution, or both.

John Quincy Adams, called a National Republican, followed. By the time Andrew Jackson was elected in 1828, those three parties had run their course.

Founding of the Modern Democratic Party

Andrew Jackson, the seventh US president, established the modern Democratic Party, first called Jacksonians, which he and other slave owners founded to keep slavery alive permanently, oppose a national bank, and push democracy over republicanism.

To justify their enslavement of other human beings and absolve themselves of blame for denying the natural rights of their slaves, slave owners had already persuaded many white Americans that black men were inherently inferior, and needed to be controlled and supported by their white slave owners.

Slave owners demonstrated their supposedly Christian good will by feeding and clothing the poor slaves.

Democrats claimed to be the party of the common man, meaning the common white man, since they viewed black men as property. A white man who wasn't as rich or important as a slave owner could feel welcome in their party.

Promoting more equality among white men (women were not included), helped Democrats gain more traction nationally for their core value of black racial inferiority.

Another goal of Andrew Jackson and his fellow Democratic slave owners was to get the American Indians out of their way and take their land, in violation of legitimate treaties.

After they passed the Indian Removal Act of 1830, they pushed out Native American Indians of the five "civilized" tribes. Possibly as many as 60-80,000 or more were removed from their homes and forced to relocate west of the Mississippi River, mostly to the Oklahoma Territory.

Thousands died during this Trail of Tears removal, which continued beyond Jackson's term, but estimates of how many Indians were removed and how many died are widely variable.

The Cherokee, Chickasaw, Choctaw, Muscogee Creek, and Seminole Indians were called civilized tribes because they were mostly farmers by then. They lived in villages, built schools, banks, and other businesses, and many had adopted the customs of white US citizens, including even the uncivilized Democratic custom of some owning slaves.

The Whig Party

The Whig Party was founded in the early 1830s to oppose what they called the tyrannical policies of Jackson, but Whigs weren't united in their opposition to slavery.

Many Whigs were abolitionists, but some agreed with the Democratic core value of black racial inferiority. Some Whigs had no problem with slavery. Others, including 13th President Millard Fillmore, disliked slavery, but didn't actively oppose it.

Democrats and Whigs

Jackson was followed by Democrat Martin Van Buren, and Whig Presidents William Henry Harrison (for only a month) and John Tyler, who was then expelled from the Whig Party.

Democrat James Polk was 11th president, then Whigs Zachary Taylor (for 16 months) and Millard Fillmore. Harrison and Taylor, the only Whig presidents ever elected, both died in office, serving only 17 months between them.

Democrats Franklin Pierce and James Buchanan served as the 14th and 15th US presidents.

Whigs, Democrats, and Compromises

During these turbulent years of expansion, dominated by Democrats from Jackson thru Buchanan, national political debate was often dominated by Whigs Henry Clay of Kentucky and Daniel Webster of Massachusetts and by Democrats John C. Calhoun of South Carolina and Stephen Douglas of Illinois.

These great orators and political leaders debated and settled many issues in Congress, but the most contentious issues were about the expansion of slavery into new territories and States.

There was no serious threat to abolish slavery, but much debate over how far the Democratic slave owners could expand its reach and strengthen their political power to perpetuate it.

The Compromise of 1850

Some of these political leaders had been involved in the Missouri Compromise of 1820 over the expansion of slavery before the Democratic and Whig Parties existed, and they continued to compromise away the human rights of black slaves.

After they agreed to the Compromise of 1850, which kept the balance between slave and free states, effectively repealed the Missouri Compromise, and established a harsh new Fugitive Slave Law, they expressed confidence that they had buried all the troubles of the nation regarding slavery.

While these great compromisers settled issues they thought were more important, they kept ignoring the fact that freedom and protection of human rights were the basis of what the United Sates was about, and the reasons for its existence and success.

The Kansas Nebraska Act

Then, Democratic Senate Majority Leader Stephen Douglas pushed the Kansas Nebraska Act of 1854 through Congress to hand Democrat slave owners a great victory by allowing whites who settled in Kansas and Nebraska to decide whether slavery would be legal. This law demonstrated the failure of democracy to protect freedom vs. constitutional republican government under which individuals possess natural rights that can't be voted away by a majority.

The Abolitionists

The Abolitionist Movement

While Democrats worked to keep slavery permanently alive and Whigs compromised, an abolitionist movement grew.

William Lloyd Garrison, Wendell Phillips, Charles Lenox Redmond, Isaac and Amy Post, James Monroe, Sojourner Truth, Harriet Beecher Stowe, Charles Sumner, and many others dedicated their efforts to abolishing slavery.

The Liberator and the *National Anti-Slavery Standard* newspapers promoted abolishing slavery, and the American Anti-Slavery Society worked to free the slaves.

Frederick Douglass, Abolitionist Leader

Frederick Douglass, who had mostly taught himself to read and write, escaped from slavery in 1838 and made his way to Massachusetts to live and find work.

Frederick Douglass received help from white and black people who wished him well, but he discovered that Democratic core values were well-accepted as far north as Massachusetts. He had to ride in segregated sections on public transportation, and was often told in public buildings, and even in a church, "We don't allow (black people) in here." [xviii]

Within a few years, Douglass was invited to join the abolitionists and tell his story. He enthusiastically used his reading, writing, and speaking skills to help the cause. Sponsored by prominent abolitionists, he embarked with others on a speaking tour of Vermont, New York, Ohio, and Indiana.

Frederick Douglass refused to help a fellow abolitionist who wanted to also promote communism, and the tour stuck to its anti-slavery message. He was warmly received by some large audiences, but by others was slandered, verbally abused, pelted with rotten eggs, and then severely beaten by a mob in Indiana.

Douglass later traveled to England and Ireland, where he was surprised to find that no one shunned him or was offended by his race, as people often were in the land of the free. When he returned, he became a prominent abolitionist, and began publishing his own newspaper in Rochester, New York in 1847.

The abolitionist movement was getting stronger, but there was still not a strong national political party to consistently stand up for the human rights of the slaves. Newspaper publisher Frederick Douglass became one of the prominent abolitionists calling for a stronger stand against slavery.

Frederick Douglass

Founding of the Modern Republican Party

Abolitionists were alarmed by the Compromise of 1850 because it enabled the expansion of slavery and included the Fugitive Slave Act, which legally bound free States to cooperate with slave owners and their bounty hunters who came into their jurisdictions, brutally kidnapped black men suspected of being escaped slaves, and hauled them away without due process.

The 1854 Kansas-Nebraska Act not only changed the balance of free vs. slave States in favor of the Democrat slave owners, but served as a warning that slavery could be forced upon the entire nation and continue perpetually unless some significant change was made.

The Republican Party was founded as the anti-slavery party in 1854 by Whigs who were dissatisfied with their party's weak stand against slavery, members of the fading Free Soil Party, and other abolitionists, shortly after Kansas-Nebraska was enacted.

Former Whig Congressman Abraham Lincoln spoke strongly against the Kansas-Nebraska Act as he campaigned for Republican congressional candidates.

Republicans nominated John C. Fremont as their presidential candidate in 1856. Democrat James Buchanan beat Fremont, but Republicans won 11 States and many seats in Congress.

Supreme Court Definition of Freedom in the Dred Scott Case

The Republican Party grew stronger after the Dred Scott decision in 1857, in which the Democrat-dominated Supreme Court ruled that a black man could never become a citizen of the United States even if he had been freed from slavery.

Democratic Chief Justice Roger Taney went to great lengths in his majority opinion to explain that the black race had always been deemed to be inferior to whites, and that black men had no rights which white men were bound to respect.

The Chief Justice wrote that if black men were allowed to claim citizenship, they would be truly free men, able to speak freely, hold assemblies, travel wherever they wanted, and to own and carry guns.

The right to bear arms defined the difference between a free man and a slave who had no such right.

Republican Abraham Lincoln vs. Democrat Stephen Douglas

Abraham Lincoln then challenged powerful Democrat Stephen Douglas for his senate seat in 1858, leading to the famous Lincoln-Douglas debates.

Lincoln argued that slavery was an immoral injustice, and against the fundamentals of civil liberty. He argued that our founders didn't create slavery in our country, and that they knew it was wrong, but didn't know how to get rid of it at the time.

Lincoln pointed out that our founders prohibited the slave trade and prohibited slavery in new territories, thinking their actions would speed its extinction. He said the battle against slavery was the same as the battle for the common rights of humanity vs. the supposed divine right of kings.

Lincoln warned that the expansion of slavery would lead it to become perpetual and national, and he strongly warned Republicans not to compromise.

Democrat Stephen Douglas defeated Lincoln in the Illinois Senate election, but Lincoln's continued fight against expansion of slavery helped him win the Republican nomination for president, which would pit him against Douglas again in 1860.

12

Civil War and Assassination

Election of 1860

Illinois Senator Stephen Douglas was the Democratic Party's presidential nominee in 1860. Despite his success in expanding slavery's grip on the country, he wasn't deemed by southern Democrats to be sufficiently strong in his devotion to slavery.

Southern Democrats nominated Vice President John Breckenridge in a separate convention. He supported slavery, but discouraged secession until after he lost the election.

John Bell of Tennessee was the Constitutional Union Party nominee. As a Whig senator, Bell had opposed the spread of slavery, but he had also opposed abolishing it. His only issue was to keep the Union together.

Abraham Lincoln was the Republican Party's candidate, facing Bell, Breckenridge and Stephen Douglas, who had defeated him two years earlier in the Illinois senate race.

Lincoln did not propose to abolish slavery at that time, promising to let it continue in States where it existed. His plan was to keep the Union together, stop the spread of slavery, and negotiate its abolishment through the Constitutional process.

Democratic slave owners threatened to split the Union if they didn't win the election, because they knew Republicans would eventually abolish slavery. If they couldn't win by the rules, Democrats would defend slavery at any cost.

All four candidates said they wanted to keep the Union together and avoid war. Democrats held such a strong grip on the country that Lincoln was the only candidate willing to risk defeat by opposing even the spread of slavery.

Lincoln won 39.7 percent of the popular vote, 18 of the 33 States, and a majority of electoral votes.

Civil War

Democrats created a separate government to protect their "right" to own slaves. The slave States, all led by Democrats, began to secede from the Union as soon as the results were clear.

By the time Lincoln took office, seven states had seceded and joined the Confederate States of America. Four more joined them when he called for Confederates to return control of federal property to the United States.

On April 12, 1861, Confederate forces attacked Ft. Sumter, South Carolina. The most devastating and destructive war to our country in US history was underway. The Civil War lasted four years, and claimed the lives of more than 600,000 Americans. Besides its cost in American lives, the war destroyed cities, towns, roads, railroads, and farm land.

Lincoln said his first duty was preserving the Union, and he intended to keep his election promise to do so without directly ending slavery. He hoped the war would end quickly, without much bloodshed. At first, slaves who escaped and ran to Union lines were sent home instead of being allowed to join the fight.

Major General George McClellan, the Union field commander, acted slowly and cautiously despite the Union's superior troop strength and Lincoln's orders to move more quickly. He was not vigorous in pursuing the enemy, and no match for Confederate General Robert E. Lee.

Jefferson Davis, president of the Confederate States, was a former US Army colonel, secretary of war, and Democratic senator from Mississippi. Confederates discouraged the Union from using black soldiers by threatening to execute them as traitors or sell them into slavery instead of treating them as prisoners of war, both of which they did in some cases.

Democrats had been so successful in promoting their core value of black racial inferiority that many leaders on the Union side believed it. Early on, both sides saw it as a "white man's war." The Union Army used black volunteers only as servants, then as construction workers, and then to hold captured forts.

Frederick Douglass, prominent abolitionist, newspaper publisher, and former slave, recruited many black volunteers to serve the Union throughout the war, including his sons.

Douglass met with Lincoln and his cabinet officers on several occasions, and Lincoln treated him as an important advisor. After Douglass asked Lincoln to use black volunteers as soldiers and advised him to treat them the same as white soldiers, the role of black recruits improved.

Abraham Lincoln
Alexander Gardner photo

Lincoln and Congress enacted a law in 1862 that freed the slaves of Confederate soldiers. Lincoln issued his Emancipation Proclamation in January 1863, permanently freeing all slaves in the Confederate States, as Frederick Douglass had encouraged.

Lincoln judged McClellan ineffective and replaced him as top field general. General George Meade led Union troops to victory at Gettysburg, then Lincoln promoted Ulysses S. Grant and made him commanding general in March 1864.

Election of 1864: Northern Democrats Support Confederates

The country was tired of the war, heavy casualties, and destruction of property. Partly due to political policies, the war didn't seem to be nearing a successful conclusion.

Democrats in the northern States tried to defeat their own country's war effort from within, claiming that Union victory was impossible. Their 1864 Chicago Platform called for ending the war and reuniting the country by effectively surrendering and embracing slavery. George McClellan, whom Lincoln had relieved of command, ran as the Democratic candidate.

John Fremont and other Republicans, frustrated that Lincoln had not supported immediate abolition, formed the Radical Democracy Party, with Fremont as their candidate.

Republicans joined with the minority of Democrats who supported the Union but didn't want to be called Republicans, under the National Union Party label. Andrew Johnson, one of those Democrats, became wartime military governor of his home State of Tennessee after Union victory there, and was chosen as Lincoln's vice presidential running mate.

War Developments

Grant's aggressive military leadership turned the tide. His top generals William Tecumseh Sherman, Philip Sheridan, and others won decisive victories. Union victory was within reach.

Among Grant's successful military strategies was that he used black volunteers as combat soldiers. Black soldiers responded with great valor and helped win battles.

The majority of Union soldiers who served and died in this war against slavery were white men. But black volunteers who were finally allowed to prove their ability on the battlefield contributed significantly to the eventual Union victory.

Others helped, too, including Harriet Tubman, who escaped slavery, led others to freedom, served as a nurse, scout, and recruiter, and led Union soldiers at least once in armed combat.

Harriet Tubman

1864 Election Result

To avoid helping Democrats defeat Lincoln and perpetuate slavery, John Fremont withdrew from the race.

Lincoln defeated McClellan, but Democrats won 45 percent of the popular vote in their attempt to defeat their own country's war effort, even without any votes from Confederate States.

Union Victory

Confederate General Robert E. Lee surrendered to Union General Ulysses S. Grant on April 9, 1865. The 13th Amendment was already in process of ratification by the States.

Assassination

Abraham Lincoln was assassinated five days later by a stage actor who supported slavery, and had heard him give a speech in which Lincoln supported granting former slaves the right to vote. He shot Lincoln in the back of his head on April 14, 1865, and Lincoln died early the next morning.

Frederick Douglass wrote that Lincoln had redeemed and regenerated our country from "the foulest crime against human nature" and called his assassination a "terrible calamity" for black Americans. [xix]

13

Freedom Amendments and Reconstruction

The Freedom Amendments

Although the US Constitution and Bill of Rights were not written to grant freedom or rights to people, the 13th, 14th, and 15th Amendments were written and ratified to free the slaves and establish their citizenship and voting rights.

Amendment XIII (13), approved by Congress before the Union victory and ratified in December 1865, abolished slavery in the United States and "any place subject to their jurisdiction."

Amendment XIV (14), ratified in July 1868, established that former slaves and their descendants were citizens of the United States and the States in which they lived, and prohibited any State from denying them equal protection under the law.

Amendment XV (15), ratified in February 1870, guaranteed that "The right of citizens of the United States to vote shall not be denied or abridged by the United States or by any State on account of race, color, or previous condition of servitude."

These Amendments overrode, superseded, and effectively replaced every word related to slavery in the US Constitution. They repaired the flaw in our foundation, and established that its protection of freedom and natural rights applies to all of us.

Reconstruction: Congress vs. the President

Democratic Vice President Andrew Johnson was sworn in as president a few hours after Lincoln died.

Johnson couldn't stop the abolition of slavery, but as a Democrat, he strongly opposed citizenship and voting rights for former slaves. His goal was to get the country back to business as usual before the Civil War with as few changes as possible.

Republicans in Congress passed Reconstruction Acts, setting up temporary military governments to protect rights and property of citizens in the former Confederate States, except in Johnson's home State of Tennessee, which had ratified the 14th Amendment and been readmitted to the Union.

States were required to draft new State constitutions, repeal the Black Codes they had passed to effectively nullify abolition, grant voting rights to black men, and ratify the 14th Amendment.

Democrat Johnson vetoed the Reconstruction Acts of the Republican Congress, and they overrode his vetoes. He issued a series of pardons to Confederate Democrats, and struggled against the Republicans in Congress over many issues.

The House impeached Johnson in 1868, and he maneuvered to gain acquittal in the Senate. Amid accusations over their motives, seven Republicans joined all the Democrats to acquit him by one vote. Some may have voted to acquit because they opposed their own president *pro tem* of the Senate, who would have then become US president. Struggles over Reconstruction continued until Johnson's term expired in March 1869.

Republican Ulysses S. Grant, former commanding general of the Union Army, won the presidential election of 1868.

Black Republicans during Reconstruction

Former slaves voted in the former Confederate States, and black voters suddenly outnumbered white voters in many local areas. Black American citizens, including former slaves, ran for office as Republicans, and many served as local officials.

Black men served as State representatives and State senators for the first time, creating Republican majorities in several State legislatures. They didn't outnumber whites, but helped Republicans outnumber white-supremacist Democrats.

Starting in 1870, twenty black Republicans served in the US House, and two in the US Senate. Among them were:

Joseph Rainey, Republican of South Carolina. Born a slave, he served during five terms in the US House from 1870-1879.

Blanche K. Bruce was elected by the Republican Mississippi Senate, and he served a full term in the US Senate from 1875-81.

47

Richard H. Cain, Republican of South Carolina, served two terms in the US House, 1873-75 and 1877-79.

John R. Lynch of Mississippi, born a slave, was speaker of the Mississippi House in 1873, and served three terms in the US House from 1874-77, and 1881-83. He also worked in the Executive Branch, held a national leadership position in the Republican Party, and wrote *The Facts of Reconstruction*, a book which provided some of the information in this chapter.

Robert Smalls, a South Carolina Republican, freed himself and other slaves by taking control of a Confederate transport ship to escape in 1862, then went on to serve several terms in the US House, 1875-1887.

Democrats repeatedly challenged the elections of black Republican legislators, preventing some from serving full terms.

Robert Smalls

The Potential Threat of "Negro Domination"

Lynch told us black men generally didn't want to dominate whites, and bore surprisingly little animosity after all the years of mistreatment they endured under slavery. They just wanted to live like other people, have a say in the government under which they lived, and be reasonably represented in government.

John R. Lynch

Democrats kept claiming that black people were inferior, and white men should still be completely in charge. John R. Lynch explained in *The Facts of Reconstruction* that Democrats fought to suppress the black vote to avoid "Negro Domination."

"Negro Domination" didn't mean whites having black people as their masters, as whites had enslaved blacks. To Democrats, black domination occurred when white men were split on an issue and the votes of black men could give one side a majority, thus enabling black men to cast the deciding votes. Democrats didn't believe a black man should have any say. [xx]

Reconstruction: Swimming Against the Democratic Tide

Republicans temporarily reconstructed political reality in the former Confederate States, but Democrats clinging to their core value of black racial inferiority blocked reconstruction of relations between white and black people.

Wealthy Democrats had used their black slaves for many years as carpenters, blacksmiths, mechanics, and other skilled laborers on their plantations. They knew black people weren't inferior, but they kept promoting that core value to less affluent whites to maintain the Democratic "party of the common man."

Many white men strongly believed it, and they had just lost a war over it. Now they were competing against "inferior" black men for work in their trades, and resented competing with them.

Democrats organized violent hate groups including the Red Shirts, the White League, and the Ku Klux Klan (KKK) to terrorize blacks and other Republicans and suppress their votes.

End of Reconstruction and Democratic Resurgence

Grant and Republicans in Congress who favored strong Reconstruction measures won the 1872 election handily.

But a financial panic in 1873, and corruption among officials appointed by Grant helped Democrats gain a mid-term victory in 1874, and Republicans began losing their ability to protect the rights of black citizens in the South.

With Democratic terrorist organizations suppressing black votes in the South during the 1876 election, Democrats won most of the former Confederate States, but counts in four States were disputed.

Democrats threatened mob violence by thousands of armed men in Washington DC if Democrat Samuel J. Tilden was not sworn in as President. But Republican Rutherford B. Hayes won by one electoral vote and was sworn in as 19th US president after an alleged compromise deal which required him to withdraw US troops, ending Reconstruction in the South.

Democrats Back in Power

Hayes had fought in the Civil War and supported Reconstruction measures in Congress. After he pulled federal troops from the South to end Reconstruction, he continued to fight for the civil rights of black Americans as president, but Democrats in the House blocked his efforts.

14

Victory for Freedom Diminished

Dark Ages for Civil Rights

After the post-war Reconstruction period ended in 1877, Democrats quickly regained political power, and Republicans lost their ability to protect the rights of black Americans.

Democrats couldn't bring back slavery, but they quickly restored white racial supremacy and Democratic political supremacy. Through unconstitutional voting restrictions, segregation, racial discrimination, and terrorism, they kept black and white Republicans from voting and holding elected offices.

By 1880, just fifteen years after the end of the Civil War, the Democratic former slave owners were back in control. Ignoring the 14th Amendment, they enacted laws to enforce segregation and racial discrimination throughout the South.

In violation of the 15th Amendment, Democrats contrived legal mechanisms to deprive black citizens of their right to vote. One example was the "grandfather clause," barring any man from voting if his grandfather had not been a registered voter.

They segregated schools, workplaces, hotels, buses, trains, and even public restrooms. Their discriminatory laws were enacted in southern States, but helped entrench the practice of segregation and racial discrimination throughout the country.

Democrats also enforced segregation and discrimination as members of white supremacist organizations including the White League, the Red Shirts, and the Ku Klux Klan (KKK), which became the main enforcement arm of their party.

Klan members in white sheets and hoods terrorized and lynched black and white Republicans. Gun control laws kept black men unable to defend themselves against KKK terrorism.

Slavery had been abolished, but former slaves and their descendants would be blocked by Democrats from living in freedom for 100 years after the Civil War. Amid US freedom and prosperity, black Americans were discriminated against, segregated, treated as second class citizens, and terrorized.

Rights of All Americans Damaged

To justify limiting the citizenship and voting rights of the former slaves and their descendants established by the 14th and 15th Amendments, Democratic leaders began to narrowly define the rights of all citizens.

They increasingly treated the Constitution as if it had been written to limit and define the rights of citizens, instead of for its true purpose, to grant limited powers to the federal government.

A Second President Assassinated

After Reconstruction ended under Hayes, Republican James Garfield served as 20th US president for only 6 months before he was assassinated. Republican Chester Arthur served the rest of his term, followed by Democrat Grover Cleveland, Republican Benjamin Harrison, and then by Cleveland again.

Civil Rights Dark Ages Continue

When the Supreme Court overturned the 1875 Civil Rights Act in 1883, Republican Chester Arthur asked Congress to pass a new law to replace it. But with a Democratic majority in the House, he couldn't persuade Congress to take action.

Republican President Benjamin Harrison, another Civil War veteran, ordered his attorney general to prosecute people who violated the voting rights of black Americans. But all-white juries of Democrats failed to convict, or even indict violators.

Harrison pressed Congress to pass a Federal Elections Bill proposed by Republican Representative Henry Lodge and Republican Senator George Hoar in 1890, requiring federal supervision of federal elections to protect black Americans in the South, but Democrats filibustered it in the Senate.

Democrat Grover Cleveland, of course, made no such effort.

Republicans repeatedly attempted to secure the rights of black Americans, while Democrats repeatedly blocked them.

Supreme Court vs. Freedom

In *US v. Cruikshank, Plessy v. Ferguson*, and other cases, the justices went beyond misinterpreting the Constitution as they twisted its words to deny black citizens their rights.

A Third President Assassinated

Republican William McKinley, serving as 25th president, became the third president to be assassinated, a few months into his second term. Less than 50 years after the anti-slavery party was founded, all three assassinated presidents were Republicans.

Growing Power of Government and the Press

Republican Theodore Roosevelt (TR) succeeded McKinley. TR was popular, but expanded government powers and the role of president. He once mistakenly claimed he had the power do anything not specifically prohibited by the Constitution.

TR exceeded Constitutional limits by attempting to solve almost every problem he saw. Some of his actions had positive effects, and he held frequent press conferences to claim credit. Although TR saw evil in the power large corporations and made headlines for "anti-trust" actions, banker JP Morgan is often credited with solving the financial panic of 1907.

McKinley and Roosevelt both wanted to stop oppression of black Americans, but backed down to the power of Democrats. TR was strongly criticized by Democrats for inviting black scientist Booker T. Washington for dinner at the White House.

TR was followed by Republican William Howard Taft, whom he strongly endorsed, until four years later.

Progressives, Democrats, and Republicans

In the early 1900s, Democratic leaders and a faction that split from the Republican Party aligned with the progressive movement, which rejected the principle of natural rights that the US Declaration of Independence and US Constitution are based upon. A progressive leader wrote that the rights of men are not absolute, but to be "determined by the legislative authority in view of the needs of that society." [xxi]

15

Socialism and Communism

It is important to understand some facts about socialism and communism because they completely oppose the principles of freedom and natural rights. We often hear their ideas proposed as solutions to our problems, and see them enacted by our federal government in defiance of individual rights.

Socialism is a theory of social organization in which the means of production, distribution, exchange, and other property is owned or controlled by the state. Economic and social activity is controlled by the social elite, theoretically for the benefit of the whole community. Socialism became popular in France in the late 1700s, and has sometimes been called a religion.

Communism goes a step beyond most socialism. Usually imposed by violent revolution, it prohibits individual ownership of property. All economic and social activity is controlled by the state, under a single political party. Communism claims to supersede any other social order and all religions.

Flashback: American Experiment in Socialism

Some of the earliest American colonists thought that sharing everything for the good of the whole community would be the best way to survive the challenges facing them. Sharing would insure that there would be plenty for everyone, they thought.

It may have been a good idea, but when the leaders imposed that plan, men didn't work as hard and women didn't help their husbands in the fields. Single men complained about having to work to support the wives and children of other men. This experiment in socialism caused a food shortage that almost starved the colony out of existence during the first winter.

The Pilgrims realized they needed a new plan, so they let each man keep what he produced. The food shortage was suddenly over. Men worked harder in the fields, and their wives voluntarily helped them. The Pilgrims could still share, but with the sharing voluntary, there was plenty of food.

This unplanned experiment has been mostly forgotten.

The Industrial Revolution

Beginning in the mid-1700s, inventions of manufacturing machinery increased industrial productivity, and changed the way people worked and lived.

Businessmen invented and bought manufacturing machinery, built factories, and hired workers. This required risking large sums of money (capital) that they had to supply from their own resources or borrow on credit, so they were called capitalists.

In Europe and England, poor serfs migrated from farms to cities because the money they could earn in factories improved their living conditions. Some came to America.

Large populations of low-income people became concentrated in European cities, and were soon as dissatisfied with life there as they had been with their lives in the country. They were still poor, but were crowded together. Many believed the capitalist factory owners were taking unfair advantage of them, and in some cases they were correct.

The Communist Manifesto

Karl Marx and Friedrich Engels published the *Manifesto of the Communist Party* in 1848, [xvii] preceded by the "Draft of a Communist Confession of Faith" by Engels. [xxiii] Marx was the primary author of this plan to fight supposed injustices through class warfare. Communist quotes here are from both sources.

Class Envy and Class Warfare

Marx divided all society into two classes, the bourgeoisie and the proletariat. The bourgeoisie were the capitalists, owners of the means of production, and employers of wage laborers. The proletariat were the wage laborers who, owning no means of production, were "reduced" to selling their labor to live.

Marx described many grievances of the factory workers, legitimate and imagined. It's always easy to find both kinds in

55

any work place, and to blame them on the employer. Laborers worked long hours, their pay was low, and their lives were hard.

Many had lived even-harder lives and might have still been living those lives as serfs if they hadn't come to the cities for better factory jobs. But it's easy to forget or ignore such facts.

Marx emotionally attacked the personal excesses and weaknesses of capitalists, to make workers envy them and to justify violent class warfare against them.

Marx wrote that the means of production--factories, money, and land--all rightfully belonged to the workers because they did the work, even though the employers had worked and risked their money to build factories and hire the workers.

His plan was for mobs of workers to overthrow capitalists by forcibly stealing their property through violent revolution. Leaders like Marx would then take control in the name of the people who thought they deserved to own everything.

He would then abolish all private ownership of property, and committees of workers would decide how to share the loot they had stolen. In other words, chaos would determine which thieves would rule as dictators over the others and their stolen property.

Marx wrote that the first step in the revolution is to raise the working class to the position of ruling class to win the battle of democracy. (Note his use of the word democracy.)

"The proletariat will use its political supremacy to wrest, by degree, all capital from the bourgeoisie, to centralise all instruments of production in the hands of the State, i.e., of the proletariat organised as the ruling class..."

After public ownership was achieved, he theorized, workers would work even more productively for the good of all.

Marx's plan boiled down to violent revolution, massive theft, and fantasy, but there was more that made it worse.

Indoctrination and Attacks on Religion and Families

After abolishing property rights, Marx wanted to free people from religion and family duties, and indoctrinate their children.

"… Communism…makes all existing religions superfluous and supersedes them."

"The charges against Communism made from a religious, a philosophical and, generally, from an ideological standpoint, are not deserving of serious examination."

Marx wrote that all children should be educated (including indoctrinated) at state expense in state establishments from the time when they can first do without maternal care.

Engels wrote, "We will only interfere in the personal relationship between men and women or with the family in general to the extent that (they would) disturb the new social order." In other words, they would interfere with families only if they were inconvenient to government rulers.

Marx described socialism as the transitional stage between revolution and communism. His steps during the transformation from socialism to communism included:

1. Abolition of private property.

2. A heavy progressive or graduated income tax.

3. Abolition of all rights of inheritance.

4. Confiscation of the property of all emigrants and rebels (anyone who didn't agree with them).

5. Centralization of credit by means of a national bank with an exclusive monopoly.

6. Centralization of the means of communication and transport in the hands of the State.

7. State control over factories and farming in accordance with a common plan.

8. Establishment of industrial armies.

The Difference between Socialism and Communism

Marx saw socialism as only partially implemented communism, and expressed disgust for elitists who set socialism as their goal.

"To this section belong economists, philanthropists, humanitarians, improvers of the condition of the working class, organisers of charity, members of societies for the prevention of cruelty to animals, temperance fanatics, hole-and-corner reformers of every imaginable kind..."

"...Socialists of this kind consider themselves far superior to all class antagonisms."

Marx wrote that communist rule must be established by revolution, but Engels wrote that when necessary, communists must cooperate with Democratic Socialists to achieve their goals.

"In America, where a democratic constitution has already been established, the communists must make the common cause with the party which will turn this constitution against the bourgeoisie (the middle class)."

The Law (of Free Men)

French economist Frederic Bastiat published *The Law*, his book about the principles of freedom vs. socialism, in 1848. Bastiat's observations about the differences included,

"Socialists look upon people as raw material to be formed into social combinations."

"(Socialists) demand the use of force in order to substitute their own inclinations for those of the human race." [xxiv]

Further Reading on the Differences

Anyone trying to understand events in our country and the world can gain insight by reading both the *Manifesto of the Communist Party* by Karl Marx and Friedrich Engels, and *The Law* by Frederic Bastiat. Both are available in public libraries, and can currently be read free online.

16

Dismantling Limits and Rights

From Limited Powers to Limited Rights

While the Supreme Court ruled as if the US Constitution had been written to limit and define the rights of citizens rather than to grant limited powers to government, presidents and Congress disregarded its limits.

The Wilson Years: A Disaster for Freedom

Former Republican President Teddy Roosevelt ran against incumbent Republican President Taft as the candidate of the Progressive Party in 1912. The split among Republicans handed victory in the three way race to Democrat Woodrow Wilson.

When Wilson took office as the 28th US president in 1913, an eight-year nightmare for the protection of natural rights had just begun. Some of it was bipartisan.

16th Amendment: The Federal Income Tax

Progressive Republicans and Democrats both played roles in this disaster for individual rights, ratified just before Wilson took office. The 16th Amendment legalized a discriminatory income tax, voided important protections in Article 1 of the Constitution and conflicted with the 4th Amendment in the Bill of Rights.

Income tax was promoted as a plan to soak the rich by taxing only a few citizens with the highest incomes (the progressive income tax in the Communist Manifesto).

The lowest rate was to be one percent on incomes over $20,000 (about $440,000 in today's inflated dollars), with the highest rate at seven percent on incomes over $500,000 ($11 million today).

Using the force of law to steal only from the most successful was a popular idea when Wilson and the Democratic Congress enacted this income tax with the Revenue Act of 1913.

At first, few even had to file. But income tax allows the federal government to interfere and meddle in every American's life, liberty and property in ways completely incompatible with the government of free men designed by our founders.

The right of Americans "to be secure in their persons, houses, papers, and effects," specifically protected by the 4th Amendment, was severely damaged by the 16th Amendment. Constant expansion of federal income tax laws since then has destroyed the personal security of all Americans.

17th Amendment: Direct Election of Senators

Ratification of the 17th Amendment in April 1913 stripped States of an important safeguard to their sovereignty. Election of US senators by State legislatures was in the Constitution to ensure that interests of citizens were represented by their States.

Wilson's Segregation of Armed Forces and Federal Offices

Wilson's support for segregation came from his upbringing and the Democratic core value of black racial inferiority. His family had owned slaves and supported the Confederacy in the Civil War during his childhood in Georgia. He couldn't own slaves any more, but he could segregate and discriminate.

Wilson ended racial integration in the US military and federal agencies. Black soldiers under Wilson were segregated, led by white officers, and kept mostly in support roles.

Wilson supported segregation of federal agencies under his cabinet. Office areas, cafeterias, and restrooms were segregated. He supported Democrat Jim Crow laws and openly regarded the Ku Klux Klan terrorists as heroic protectors of society.

The Federal Reserve

Congress has the constitutional duty and power to coin (and print) money, regulate the value thereof, and to borrow money on the credit of the United States.

After several financial panics, Congress and Wilson created the Federal Reserve in 1913, transferring this responsibility to a committee of private bankers and federal bureaucrats, although Congress had no constitutional authority to transfer this duty.

The intent of the Federal Reserve was to supervise and regulate banking institutions and conduct monetary policy to avoid problems like the Great Depression, which it actually helped trigger, and then exacerbated.

The Federal Reserve actually colludes with presidents and Congress to give us a false sense of security by artificially manipulating our economy to hide the damage their spending and other policies are doing to our freedom.

Economics Professor Thomas Sowell and former US Congressman Ron Paul have been leading advocates for reforming or completely eliminating the Federal Reserve.

Implementing Marxism

Wilson and the Democratic majority in Congress increased federal control over banking, railroads and farming, elevated the rights of union bosses, and enacted a progressive income tax, all steps that Marx had laid out in the Communist Manifesto.

Administrative Law

Our founders didn't create Congress to micromanage the lives of citizens. The Constitution granted Congress limited powers with the exclusive power to legislate to ensure that the people and States would never be subject to laws not carefully reviewed and voted on by their representatives and senators.

But when Congress legislates solutions to so many problems not under their constitutional authority, writing that many laws can become tedious and time-consuming. So Congress has turned over many of its legislative duties to the executive branch. This unconstitutional practice increased during the Wilson years.

Administrative Law, supported by government force as if it were legislation, is written by appointed bureaucrats in federal agencies, violating the separation of powers by effectively allowing one branch to both write and enforce the laws, and act as judges in many cases.

Administrative law usurps the powers of States and limits individual freedom. There are so many administrative laws now that it's impossible to know all the laws that regulate us.

World War I

World War I began in Europe in July 1914. The US was drawn into the war in April 1917, and helped end it in November 1918. Of the 16 million killed, 54,000 were Americans. The treaty negotiated by Wilson was not approved by the Senate, but it led to some of the causes of World War II.

During World War I, Wilson and Congress enacted the first involuntary military draft with the Selective Service Act of 1917.

Unions and Strikes

Wilson favored unions, but opposed strikes during the war. To avoid a fight with railroad union bosses just months before entering the world war, Wilson and the Democratic Congress passed the Adamson Act, the first federal law imposing hours and pay regulations on private companies, although they had no constitutional authority to enact such a law.

18th Amendment: Prohibition

The 18th Amendment, ratified in 1919, deprived citizens and States of their rights by prohibiting the manufacture, sale, and transportation of alcoholic beverages. Prohibition helped build organized crime into a powerful force, as citizens continued to drink alcohol. It was repealed in 1933 by the 21st Amendment.

19th Amendment: Freedom for Women

After all the dismantling of freedom and individual rights during the Wilson years, a new freedom amendment was ratified.

Since the 1840s, women's rights advocates including Sojourner Truth, Amy Post, Harriet Tubman, Susan B. Anthony, Elizabeth Cady Stanton, Frederick Douglass, Wendell Phillips, and others had been calling for voting rights for women.

The 19th Amendment, establishing the right of women to vote, passed Congress in June 1919, was ratified by the States, and became effective in August 1920. Ironically, Wilson's wife was unofficially running the executive branch during that time, after he suffered a stroke.

17

Prosperity between Disaster and Depression

Normalcy and Recovery

When Republican Warren Harding took office as 29th US president in 1921, the economy was in a post-war recession and debt was high. Harding's policy of Normalcy was to let US economic freedom work without interference from government.

Harding and the Republican Congress cut federal spending, lowered taxes, and instituted a federal budgeting process which has been followed ever since. The economy recovered quickly.

Harding's Civil Rights Efforts

While the Ku Klux Klan was experiencing a resurgence after encouragement from Democrat Woodrow Wilson, and while few black Americans could vote, Republican Warren Harding spoke in favor of civil rights legislation. He advocated educational and economic equality, and voting rights for black Americans. The Dyer anti-lynching bill he promoted passed the House, but was defeated by a Democratic filibuster in the Senate.

Harding died suddenly of a suspected stroke or heart attack in August 1923.

Quiet Prosperity

Republican Calvin Coolidge, often called Silent Cal, succeeded Harding as 30th US president. According to Amity Shlaes, author of an acclaimed Coolidge biography, he was a more assertive president than his nickname might imply. [xxv]

Coolidge and the Republican Congress kept federal spending low, paid down the national debt, and repeatedly lowered taxes until only a small percentage of the wealthiest had to pay income taxes by 1927.

This time of great prosperity was called the Roaring Twenties. The stock market grew. The middle class expanded rapidly, and people bought cars and radios. Entertainment flourished. New medicines were developed. Millions of black Americans were able to move north for better jobs and schools.

Coolidge's Civil Rights Efforts

Coolidge often spoke to promote civil rights for black Americans, and repeatedly called for anti-lynching laws. Like Harding, he couldn't get his proposals past threats of Democratic filibusters in the Senate, but the Ku Klux Klan lost some of its influence during his term.

He signed the Indian Citizenship Act of 1924, establishing US citizenship for all American Indians. In a commencement address at Howard University, he thanked black Americans for their service in World War I and their contributions to US society, despite having to face blatant discrimination.

An example of his attitude toward the rights of black Americans was in a reply he wrote to a white citizen who claimed that this is a "white man's country" and criticized Coolidge for promoting civil rights:

[As president, I feel] "...a responsibility for living up to the traditions and maintaining the principles of the Republican Party. Our Constitution guarantees equal rights to all our citizens, without discrimination on account of race or color. I have taken my oath to support that Constitution." [xxvi]

Popular Silence

Calvin Coolidge might have been known as a silent president because he didn't give long speeches, but he was popular. When a Republican senator ran against him as a Progressive during his bid for a full term in 1924, Coolidge didn't even campaign very aggressively after the sudden, unexpected death of his young son. But in a three-way race and the Republican Party split, he won 35 States and a clear majority of the popular vote.

Many Americans were shocked and disappointed in 1927 when Coolidge famously announced "I do not choose to run for President in 1928." Calvin Coolidge finished his term in 1929 as President of a prosperous country.

Change Was Coming

Republican Herbert Hoover, secretary of commerce under Harding and Coolidge, won the election of 1928 to become the 31st US president in 1929. Coolidge didn't strongly endorse Hoover because he had doubts about his judgement.

If Coolidge had run in 1928, the Great Depression may have never happened. It could have been reduced to a recession, and ended in just a year or two. Coolidge died about two months before the end of what would have been his second full term, but that might have been long enough to avoid Hoover's misguided policies and the destruction of freedom that followed under FDR.

18

Destruction of Limits, Depression, and War

The Great Depression: Misery and Lies

The Great Depression of 1929 to 1941 was a time of great misery and hopelessness in the United States.

Americans born after the Depression have been taught all our lives that it was caused by a stock market crash resulting from a great failure of capitalism, and government inaction.

We've been taught that the Depression was finally ended by President Franklin D. Roosevelt, (FDR), with his New Deal.

The misery and hopelessness were real, but almost everything else we've been taught about the Depression is false. This fiction was harmful to the people who believed it then, and can be more harmful to us if we continue to believe it today.

The falsehoods are still taught today, but the truth about the Great Depression can be found in "Great Myths of the Great Depression," [xxvii] by economist Lawrence W. Reed, and in works by Milton Friedman and Anna Schwartz, Jim Powell, Burton W. Folsom, Hans Sennholz, Thomas Sowell, Murray Rothbard, Walter Williams, Amity Shlaes, John T. Flynn, and others.

The Real Causes and the Cure

First of all, capitalism didn't fail; government manipulation of capitalism is what failed.

The stock market crash and government inaction didn't cause the Depression. Government action triggered the crash, and extreme government overreactions under Hoover and FDR turned the resulting recession into a depression.

FDR's New Deal didn't end the Great Depression. FDR and Congress turned a depression that could have been overcome in a year or two into more than a decade of misery and hopelessness by imposing socialist "solutions" that followed steps from the

Communist Manifesto, whether intentionally or not. The New Deal actually prevented recovery until World War II intervened.

With the help of the Supreme Court justices he bullied, FDR permanently damaged our federal government's ability to protect the freedom and rights of all Americans.

World War II ended the Great Depression. We've recovered from the war, but the destruction of freedom begun by FDR's New Deal of socialism continues to hurt us today.

The Stock Market Crash of 1929

Business cycles experience natural highs and lows in a free market, but government actions triggered the stock market crash of 1929. The Federal Reserve suddenly tightened the money supply it had earlier inflated, almost doubling interest rates in just over 18 months. Newspapers reported just before the crash that Congress was ready to pass a steep tariff rate increase that would disrupt foreign trade, and investors panicked.

The crash was bad, but it wasn't the market's first, and it could have been survived without causing a major depression.

Government Overreaction turned it into a Depression

Far from taking no action, Republican President Herbert Hoover and the Republican Congress took all the wrong actions by rapidly increasing taxes and spending. Despite pleas and warnings from over a thousand economists, they enacted the Smoot-Hawley Tariff in 1930, designed to lower unemployment.

Economist Thomas Sowell wrote that unemployment rose to 9 percent just after the crash, dropped to 6.3 percent just before the tariff increase, then rose to double digits within 5 months after, and stayed there throughout the 1930s. The tariff killed jobs, wiped out US agricultural markets, drove the stock market even lower, and turned the recession into a depression. [xxviii]

Then, as economist Lawrence W. Reed wrote, the Federal Reserve raised interest rates again. Hoover and Congress doubled income tax rates, and increased spending on relief efforts. Hoover and labor unions pushed employers to keep wages artificially high, which caused even more layoffs.

For every action that could have helped the economy recover, they took the opposite action, making a bad situation worse. Their actions also contributed to the sinking world economy, making US recovery even more difficult.

FDR's New Deal: Give Up Your Freedom

But then it got worse. Democratic President Franklin D. Roosevelt (FDR) took office in 1933 with an anti-business Democratic Congress, turned what could have been a short depression into a decade of misery, and destroyed much of our federal government's ability to protect the rights of Americans.

FDR won the 1932 election by promising to balance the federal budget, cut spending 25 percent, keep US currency on the gold standard, and stop government interference with private enterprise. His campaign promises could have set the economy on a course for recovery. But as soon as he was sworn in as President, he did exactly the opposite of what he had promised.

Unemployment rose to over 24 percent, and much higher in some parts of the country. FDR's policies kept the average near 20 percent for the rest of the 1930s.

Roosevelt's Abuses of Power Deepened the Depression

FDR and Congress increased spending even more, devalued the dollar, ordered confiscation of gold from private citizens, interfered with businesses, treated free enterprise as an enemy, and made recovery more difficult. Instead of helping banks recover, FDR blamed the Depression on the bankers, and caused thousands of banks to close and go out of business forever.

Roosevelt's Agriculture Adjustment Administration (AAA) raised taxes and purposely destroyed fields of cotton, wheat, and corn. They slaughtered millions of cattle, pigs, and sheep in their attempts to artificially prop up prices while many Americans didn't have enough to eat.

FDR's National Recovery Administration (NRA) destroyed a mild recovery that had begun in spite of his actions, by restricting business hours and imposing arbitrary price controls that blocked recovery.

His enforcers battered down factory doors after hours, harassed owners, interrogated workers, and confiscated business accounting records in their attempts to find violators working longer hours or charging less than the NRA had dictated.

Instead of creating real jobs, Roosevelt's Civil Works Administration (CWA) hired actors to give free shows and put millions on the federal payroll doing make-work jobs like picking up pieces of paper, raking leaves, and scaring birds away from public parks and monuments.

FDR and Congress enacted minimum wage laws that priced many lower-paid workers completely out of the labor market, quickly putting 500,000 black Americans out of work.

The National Labor Relations Act gave legal privileges and immunities to labor unions, and made almost anything an employer could do to defend himself from the union bosses an "unfair labor practice." [xxix]

Their National Labor Relations Board (NLRB) still denies employers and non-union workers equal protection under the law by elevating the rights of union bosses above theirs.

Union bosses legally steal from workers in government jobs and many private corporations today by forcing anyone who wants a job to join a union and pay union dues, which employers must deduct from their pay and turn over to the union bosses, who use them to support Democratic political campaigns.

Unions went on a rampage of violent strikes, seized factories, and destroyed the property of the employers, helping them more than double union membership.

Jim Powell, author of *FDR's Folly*, wrote, "FDR appeared to be utterly ignorant of economics. He seemed willing to try practically anything as long as it involved more government control over the economy. He was apparently unaware that such policies had been tried before in many other countries—and failed." [xxx]

Every time the economy began to recover despite damage done by the New Deal, FDR made the Depression worse. With the strength of his support in Congress, the Supreme Court appeared to be the only force that could stand in his way.

The Supreme Court finally stopped his NRA, AAA, and a few of FDR's other programs in 1935 and 1936 by ruling them unconstitutional.

You Can Fool Most of the People Some of the Time

FDR won the 1936 election in a landslide, while voters deceived by his socialist actions gave him his strongest Democratic majorities in Congress.

Democrats controlled the Senate with a 77 percent majority and the House with 76 percent. He was re-elected with Democratic majorities again in 1940 and 1944. Election results allowed FDR to rule almost as a dictator, and he did.

FDR Bullies Supreme Court to Defeat the US Constitution

Despite their absurd ruling in *US v. Butler* that enumerated powers granted to Congress by the US Constitution didn't limit anything, the Supreme Court didn't give FDR a free pass until he bullied them in retaliation for ruling against his NRA and AAA.

After his overwhelming re-election in 1936, he proposed legislation that would let him appoint extra Supreme Court justices who supported him, to break the Court's ability to uphold the Constitution against his will.

There were public protests over his plan, but the Supreme Court justices apparently believed he could crush their authority, and they were intimidated by his political power.

Under duress from this threat, the Supreme Court ruled 7-2 in the 1937 *Helvering v. Davis* case that FDR's unconstitutional Social Security program was constitutional.

The two justices who voted against it were apparently too intimidated by FDR's power to even publish dissenting opinions. The Constitution's ability to protect our freedom was broken.

Tyranny of the Democratic Majority

Why did Americans keep re-electing FDR? He was a great speaker and a great salesman who communicated effectively and often. He sold Americans on the idea that he was a champion of the people, and that more action was always needed. He kept their hope alive as he destroyed their freedom.

When people are desperate, it's easy to demonize someone who is better off. FDR demonized successful businessmen and capitalism much as Stalin demonized the rich in Russia and Hitler demonized Jews. But FDR didn't murder the people he demonized. He used democracy and socialist policies to destroy their freedom, and he attempted to murder capitalism.

The Good, among the Bad and the Ugly

World War II threatened the security of Americans and the future of civilization. To his credit, FDR rallied Americans and was seen as a strong national leader during a frightening and devastating war, and he chose the military leaders who led US troops to victory.

Civil Rights for Black Americans Suffered

Unlike fellow Republicans Harding and Coolidge, Herbert Hoover did nothing to promote equal rights for black Americans. In fact, Hoover signed the Davis Bacon Act of 1931, which still inflates costs of government projects, and protected white union workers from having to compete with black workers.

Then FDR's NRA and minimum wage policies put hundreds of thousands of black Americans out of work. Walter Williams has written that the NRA was lampooned at the time as meaning "Negro run around" or "Negroes ruined again."

The US military under FDR was segregated and the racial discrimination so blatant that it helped inspire General Dwight Eisenhower to promote civil rights legislation later as president.

FDR admirers excuse his actions by saying that military segregation never came up during his terms, and that he didn't promote anti-lynching laws while Democrats were terrorizing black Americans as members of the Ku Klux Klan because it couldn't have passed in the Democratic Congress anyway.

As with the Great Depression, FDR wasn't the solution for racial discrimination; he was a big part of the problem.

19

The Record of Socialism and Communism

Theory vs. Reality

"From each according to his ability, and to each according to his need," was the famous slogan popularized by Karl Marx.

Many are attracted to socialism and communism because sharing everything sounds great. It may be if voluntary, but living under a socialist or communist government is not so great. In real life, socialism and communism require strong, repressive governments to enforce their rule. They crush personal freedom, produce poverty, death, and despair, and don't really share.

After socialists gain control, it becomes almost impossible to restore freedom because the leaders can arbitrarily use the full force of government to disarm the people and maintain control.

During the last 100 years, the people of Russia, China, Germany, North Korea, Cuba, and other countries have lived under socialist and communist regimes. They overthrew some oppressive rulers, but their communist and socialist rulers were more oppressive, killing millions to gain and maintain control.

Communist Revolution in Russia

The Bolshevik Revolution began in Russia in 1917. After the Bolsheviks murdered the Czar, his wife and their children, they set about establishing a socialist workers' paradise based on communism. Their central committee took control over the lives of all Russians, but no paradise of any sort was ever established.

After a power struggle among the communists, Josef Stalin emerged as their leader and ruled as an iron-fisted dictator until he died in 1953. Stalin eventually ruled not only Russia, but much of Eastern Europe as leader of the Union of Soviet Socialist Republics (USSR). Stalin's use of government force to keep the people under his control claimed at least 20 million lives, and probably more than twice that many.

The Soviet Union finally collapsed under its own weight in the 1980s with a strong push from US President Ronald Reagan. Russian citizens are now free to vote in elections, but are far from free. The people who count the votes can still make the decisions. Vladimir Putin, Russia's president / ruler today, was an officer of the former USSR's secret police (KGB).

Many Americans today think of communism as benign. We forget the past, and don't recognize the connection when our own politicians promise to "tax the rich" and "redistribute the wealth."

National Socialist Workers (NAZI) Party in Germany

Adolf Hitler of the National Socialist Workers (NAZI) Party became Prime Minister of Germany in 1934. Communists and socialists claim Nazis were far different from them, but Nazis were just a different brand of socialists. Compare the Nazi promises Hitler made to the German people in 1933 to Marx's Communist Manifesto, written in Germany 85 years earlier.

Marx wrote that all property of foreigners and rebels (anyone who resisted) should be confiscated and that the class of people who owned businesses should be brought down.

Hitler initially needed support from business owners. Demonizing Jews focused his hatred and crimes against a minority who were well represented among business owners, instead of against all of them.

Hitler claimed that Jews weren't really Germans, making them both foreigners and members of the oppressive upper class in his estimation. He leveraged both class envy and religious hatred to help him get away with killing Jews, stealing their wealth, and using it to help him gain more control.

Hitler's brand of socialism was different from Stalin's communism. Hitler murdered more than six million Jews while causing the deaths of 10 to 20 million people. Stalin murdered about twice as many people, but "only" about a million of them were Jews because Stalin didn't focus on committing genocide. He just murdered anyone he deemed inconvenient to him. Neither Hitler nor Stalin created a paradise for anyone.

The US led the free world to halt Hitler's genocide in 1945, with the help of Russia. When Americans think of socialism today, they rarely think of its connection with Hitler's socialism.

North vs. South Korea

North Korea became the "Democratic People's Republic of Korea" in 1948 after occupation by the Soviet Union following World War II. Despite its deceptive official name, North Korea remains a poverty-stricken communist dictatorship in the tradition of Stalin, but under one ruling family. Its people have lived as virtual slaves under three generations of brutal, violent, mentally deranged, autocratic dictators.

South Korea, which was occupied by US troops after the war, became an independent, constitutional republic. South Korea is a thriving, free country and important US ally today.

The "Peoples Republic" of China

In 1949, after a Chinese Civil War that lasted over 20 years, Mao Tse-tung, now called Mao Zedong, declared the "People's Republic of China" (PRC). Mao's brand of communism was imported directly from Russia. Like Stalin, Mao was a ruthless dictator who clung to power for life. It has been estimated that Mao was responsible for killing 50 million Chinese people, perhaps many more, to gain and maintain control.

Under communism, China remained severely impoverished until recently, except Hong Kong, which was under British control for most of the last 100 years, and Taiwan, which has survived decades of threats from the communist mainland PRC to remain free. Both have thrived while free from communism.

After decades of third-world poverty under Mao and since his 1976 death, China has gained significant economic strength, much of it from trade with the U.S., and from allowing limited capitalist-style freedom in certain parts of the country.

While China's financial strength has grown for its leaders, they exercise almost unlimited control over the lives of the people, even forcing women to have abortions against their will. Most Chinese families are allowed to have only one child.

"Republic" of Cuba

In 1959, Fidel Castro overthrew the corrupt president of Cuba to become the country's communist dictator. He has kept Cubans impoverished and effectively enslaved since, turning over most powers to his brother after he suffered a stroke a few years ago. Many Cubans have died trying to escape his rule.

US Union Bosses and Socialists

The industrial revolution was met with strikes, violence, and a socialist union movement beginning in the late 1800s.

Union leaders were also leaders in the Socialist Party of America, the Social Democratic Party, and the Socialist Labor Party. Eugene Debs ran for president five times as a Socialist.

Some union bosses saw themselves as part of a worldwide revolution against private ownership and free enterprise, and maintained contact with Russian communists, whom they saw as their comrades during the 1917 Bolshevik Revolution.

Bill Haywood was acquitted in his trial for murder in union-related violence, but later convicted of espionage. He fled to Russia in 1921, served as labor advisor to Lenin's Bolshevik government, and lived in Russia for the rest of his life.

Later, many union bosses claimed to be anti-communists.

Wilson, FDR, and Beyond

Woodrow Wilson opposed strikes during World War I. But by the time FDR took office, union bosses and other socialists had joined with the Democrats, as predicted by Marx and Engels.

FDR's socialist New Deal policies might as well have been written by Karl Marx. They didn't cure the Great Depression, which could have probably been ended quickly or prevented by following the Constitution and allowing free enterprise to work.

The New Deal subjected the American people to a decade of unnecessary misery, and FDR's destruction of the Constitution's ability to protect our freedom began a chain of events which is destroying our freedom, our country, and our way of life today.

20

Starting to Overcome Segregation

Steps toward Freedom

When FDR died in April 1945, World War II was ending, and the war had mostly ended the Great Depression.

Democrat Harry S Truman succeeded FDR as 33rd US president. US use of atomic bombs ended the war, and the resumption of international trade brought about by the war was helping the economy recover.

The Republican-led Congress passed the Taft-Hartley Act of 1947 over Truman's veto, with help from some Democrats, to restore a few rights of employers and individual workers that were repressed by the National Labor Relations Act of 1935.

The National Association for the Advancement of Colored People (NAACP), founded in 1909, the National Urban League, founded in 1910, and the Congress of Racial Equality (CORE), founded in 1941, called for new laws to enforce the 14th and 15th Amendments, and filed lawsuits under existing laws.

Truman signed an executive order in 1948 to finally begin reversing Democrat Woodrow Wilson's segregation of the US military more than 30 years earlier.

Republican Dwight David Eisenhower, also called "Ike," was elected 34th US president in 1952. As US Army general and supreme commander of US and all Allied Forces in Europe during World War II, Ike had entrusted black soldiers with important combat roles, and he made a point of thanking them for their valiant service in Army combat units.

As President, Eisenhower implemented racial integration of US forces, and said he was embarrassed by racial discrimination he saw in train stations and other public accommodations within our country.

After NAACP member Rosa Parks was arrested for refusing to give up her bus seat to a white passenger, Reverend Martin Luther King, Jr. (MLK) and Reverend Ralph Abernathy led the Montgomery Bus Boycott of 1955-1956, which led to court decisions striking down the Democrat bus segregation laws.

King preached non-violent methods, and his supporters followed his lead. Democrats who controlled the city and State governments reacted with stronger enforcement of segregation laws, while their Ku Klux Klan supporters reacted with violence against peaceful protesters and other black citizens.

King was arrested and his home was attacked, but he never gave up. His boycott didn't end racial discrimination, but it helped dismantle segregation and focused national attention on the Jim Crow laws and the violence to which Democrats were subjecting black people.

Brown v. the Board and US Troops

NAACP attorney Thurgood Marshall won a huge victory when the 1954 Supreme Court ruling in *Brown v. the Board of Education* overturned the Democratic Supreme Court's 1896 "separate but equal" ruling.

Marshall won the unanimous decision, in which the Supreme Court finally upheld the 14th Amendment to strike down the Democratic laws segregating public schools, even though the majority of the justices on the 1954 Court had also been appointed by Democrats.

But the battle against segregation was far from over. Democratic Governor Orval Faubus of Arkansas used National Guard troops to enforce segregation by blocking black students from attending Little Rock Central High School in 1957.

Republican President Eisenhower met with Faubus and asked him to let the seven students register. When Faubus refused, Eisenhower sent federal troops, nationalized the Arkansas National Guard (placing them under his command), and kept troops there to insure the safety of the students for the rest of the school year.

First Civil Rights Law since Reconstruction

Also in 1957, Eisenhower proposed the first federal civil rights legislation to become law since Reconstruction. Democratic Senate Majority Leader Lyndon Johnson opposed it, held up its passage, and weakened its provisions. But Democrats finally ended their filibuster and it passed.

Eisenhower's Civil Rights Act of 1957 established a Civil Rights section of the Justice Department and a federal Civil Rights Commission, focused primarily on protecting the voting rights of black Americans and investigating discrimination.

Dwight David Eisenhower

More Nonviolence Met with Violence

In 1957, Reverend Martin Luther King, Jr. (MLK) founded the Southern Christian Leadership Conference (SCLC) with Reverend Ralph Abernathy, Reverend Charles K. Steele, Reverend Joseph Lowery and others. They began to use a strategy of non-violent civil disobedience to desegregate buses throughout the south.

King, Abernathy, Reverend Fred Shuttlesworth, and other brave men led non-violent protests that made progress toward dismantling segregation. Their peaceful actions repeatedly overcame actions by Democratic public officials and the violence of their party's enforcement arm, the KKK.

A KKK mob attacked Shuttlesworth with brass knuckles, beat him with chains, and stabbed his wife for attempting to register their children in a white Birmingham school in 1957.

Each time the civil rights leaders were attacked, beaten and jailed, their movement gained more strength and more support. By 1960, a growing number of white Americans were as tired as Eisenhower was of the segregation and racial discrimination to which Democrats were subjecting black Americans.

Lunch Counter Sit-Ins

In February 1960, four black students sat down at a segregated lunch counter in a Woolworth's Department Store in Greensboro, North Carolina. They were refused service because of their race, but remained in their seats until the store closed. More students joined them the next day and the day after. The lunch counter was peacefully desegregated a few months later.

Eisenhower spoke to encourage the students. The sit-ins continued at other lunch counters through the South until 1965.

Convinced that enforcement of voting rights was the most important key to ending discrimination, Eisenhower proposed a stronger civil rights bill in 1960. His new bill authorized federal government inspection of local voter registrations and provided for stronger enforcement to protect the voting rights of black Americans. The act established penalties for interfering with a person's attempt to register or vote.

Democratic Senate Majority Leader Lyndon Johnson blocked this bill, too, held up its passage, and weakened its provisions. But Johnson wanted to soften his segregationist reputation before the presidential election. The filibuster ended, and the bill passed to become the Civil Rights Act of 1960.

Race Reality in the 1950s and 1960s

After a long history of slavery and 100 years of segregation, the Democratic Party's core value of black racial inferiority was more blatant and accepted in American life than it is today.

During a 1962 Boy Scout hike at the Civil War battlefield in Perryville, Kentucky, a white boy from Ohio was surprised to see a restroom marked "Gentlemen," and another marked "Colored." When he asked a Boy Scout leader about it, the man shrugged and said that's just the way things were "down South."

Many whites believed black people should be treated equally, but regarded the peaceful protestors as wanting equality too quickly. MLK didn't agree that 100 years after the end of slavery was too quickly. Many white people weren't afraid of his demands for equality, but afraid that he would be killed.

21

The Election of 1960

A Pivotal Election

Like the 1860 election 100 years earlier, the 1960 election was of pivotal importance to the freedom of black Americans and the future of all Americans. But although the consequences would be substantial, issues concerning freedom weren't central to the election campaigns, compared to their dominance in 1860.

The Man Who Would Be Most Powerful

Lyndon B. Johnson (LBJ) lived his life in pursuit of one goal, the acquisition and exercise of power. He wasn't driven by any cause, ideology, political philosophy, or belief. His lust was for power itself. LBJ wanted control over other people, and he did whatever it took to acquire that power.

LBJ was a Democrat because Democrats dominated State and national elections, and he accepted the Democratic core values of segregation and black racial inferiority. He started by working in a political campaign in Texas to make connections, and then became an aide to a Democratic US representative.

He quickly made friends with aides to other members of Congress and used them to make contact with some of the most powerful men in Washington, including Vice President John Nance Garner, House Speaker Sam Rayburn, and President Franklin D. Roosevelt.

He won election to the House in 1937 at age 28, on a New Deal platform. From there, he became a trusted political aide to FDR, whose ability to manipulate and control people made him a hero to LBJ. At that time, FDR was running the country almost as a dictator. Johnson may not have cared much about FDR's policies, but they helped him gain power. FDR commissioned him as a Navy officer during World War II and gave him special privileges, enabling him to report directly to the president.

LBJ won his 1948 election to the Senate in a way described as raising election fraud to a new level in Texas. [xxxi] Some called it brazen thievery.

After two years of "courting" segregationist Richard Russell and other powerful Senate Democrats, LBJ became Senate majority whip. In two more years, he was Senate minority leader, and two years later, he became Senate majority leader.

On any issue, LBJ would take whatever position would help him gain power. The Democratic Senate majority leader seemed to care most about how his position would serve his lust for power.

Once he made his decision, LBJ would become an extreme advocate of his position. He knew the ideologies, beliefs, wants, needs, strengths, and weaknesses of fellow senators, Republicans and Democrats. He knew how they might be effectively bribed, threatened, rewarded, or blackmailed, and he didn't hesitate to use any or all of those methods to get his way.

He was exceptionally well prepared when he gave each of them the Johnson "treatment" in rapid-fire fashion. He had a reputation for winning, and making any deal necessary to win.

As Senate majority leader, LBJ led the Democrats who opposed the Civil Rights Acts of 1957 and 1960, but he devised a strategy to play both sides in 1960. He strongly supported the segregationists who were his power base, but after he helped them weaken the bill, he got them to end their filibuster and let it pass, to soften his segregationist reputation just prior to the Democratic National Convention.

JFK: The Only Man Who Defeated LBJ

John F. Kennedy, called JFK, was a war hero who had been injured in World War II, and his older brother had been killed in action. He was committed to serving his family and his country.

As a senator from Massachusetts, JFK had accepted the Democratic core value of black racial inferiority, but also held the Republican view that black Americans had natural rights that should be protected. He was said to favor stronger civil rights legislation, but he didn't favor it enough to publicly challenge his majority leader. He avoided making civil rights an issue by quietly supporting LBJ and his other fellow Democrats.

Both he and LBJ wanted the Democratic presidential nomination, but JFK was better prepared for that contest and his support was stronger. JFK won the nomination at least partly because northern Democrats were concerned that LBJ's strong segregationist image might cost the party votes.

National media exposure had begun to shine the light on the Democratic Party's strong and consistent opposition to the anti-lynching laws and civil rights acts proposed by Republicans. They didn't want black Americans to become their equals under the law, but some Democrats were becoming embarrassed by their party's segregationist image.

LBJ was surprised and disappointed to lose the nomination, but he quickly recovered and planned his next steps to serve his lust for power. Despite their strong mutual dislike for each other, JFK offered LBJ the vice-presidential nomination. Was JFK's offer coerced, or was it made to balance the ticket?

Either way, LBJ surprised many by quickly accepting the nomination for a much less powerful position than he held as Senate majority leader. He was able to also run in the race to retain his Senate seat.

The General Election

Richard Nixon, Eisenhower's vice president, was the Republican candidate. JFK and Nixon knew each other well, and had a friendly relationship. They shared many of the same political views, and had developed a mutual respect for each other. During the campaign, each claimed that he would better defend the world against the spread of communism.

JFK favored civil rights legislation supporting more federal intervention. Nixon had helped Eisenhower promote federal protection of black voting rights, while JFK had quietly helped LBJ oppose that protection. But the issue of civil rights was not among the central issues in either candidate's campaign.

During the campaign, LBJ began to dramatically transform his image. His segregationist reputation had cost him the presidential nomination, but he wouldn't let it stop him from eventually gaining the ultimate power he wanted. He changed his position 180 degrees to keep it from holding him back again. LBJ suddenly began to project an image for himself as an ardent supporter of civil rights legislation.

In a close election, JFK defeated Nixon to become the 35th US president. LBJ was elected vice president, and he was also re-elected to his Senate seat, so he could have maintained his position of power if he hadn't been elected to serve just a heartbeat away from his ultimate goal, the presidency.

22

A Fleeting Victory for Freedom

Camelot, They Thought

The first two years of JFK's presidency were occupied by the Bay of Pigs Invasion, Cold War with the Soviet Union, the Cuban Missile Crisis, early US involvement in Vietnam, taxing and spending issues, and conflicts over East and West Berlin.

The press was in love with the young president with a full head of hair, his strange Boston accent, and the Kennedy family. They treated him as if he were a movie star. The struggle for civil rights continued, but JFK kept his distance.

The Continuing Struggle for Civil Rights

In the spring of 1961, Congress of Racial Equality (CORE) founder James Farmer organized racially integrated Freedom Rides through southern cities on Greyhound and Trailways buses to demonstrate the peaceful exercise of equal rights. The riders were repeatedly met with violent attacks, their bus tires were slashed, and one of their buses was firebombed.

Another group of freedom riders led by Diane Nash of the Student Nonviolent Coordinating Committee (SNCC) was met with violence in Birmingham and harassed by police under Democratic Public Safety Commissioner Bull Connor.

Altogether, several hundred riders were violently attacked, harassed, and jailed by police under the control of Democratic public officials there and in other cities.

The sit-ins at segregated lunch counters continued.

In September 1962, Democratic Governor Ross Barnett enforced segregation by blocking black student James Meredith from entering the University of Mississippi. After weeks of legal motions and negotiations, Democratic President Kennedy reluctantly followed Republican Eisenhower's precedent by taking control of the Mississippi National Guard and sending federal troops to protect Meredith from JFK's fellow Democrat.

In April 1963, Reverend King was jailed in Birmingham, after public safety officials led by Democrat Bull Connor used fire hoses and police dogs to attack non-violent black demonstrators, including children.

On June 11, 1963, JFK was pressed into action again, as Democratic Governor George Wallace enforced segregation at the University of Alabama. Wallace finally stepped aside after JFK took control of the Alabama National Guard and again sent federal troops to protect the black students.

Just after midnight that night, NAACP organizer Medgar Evers was shot in the back and killed as he stood in his own front yard in Jackson, Mississippi.

JFK apparently felt he had to take action. On June 19, 1963, he sent a proposal to the House of Representatives that would become the basis for the Civil Rights Act of 1964.

Martin Luther King, Jr.

The Speech and the Dream

On August 28, 1963, one of the greatest Americans who ever lived also took action. Reverend Martin Luther King, Jr. stood in front of more than 200,000 black and white Americans in the shadows of the Lincoln Memorial in Washington, D.C. In one of the most famous speeches in American history, he asked all Americans to help secure freedom and equal rights for black Americans. King spoke for about 15 minutes, and said more than most politicians say in 15 years of speeches.

King told Americans he dreamed of a day when all of us, black and white, would share the freedom and justice of our great country; a day when children would be judged not by the color of their skin, but by the content of their character. Many Americans heard his words, and were inspired by his dream.

More Murders and Oppression

But the deadly violence got uglier. Ku Klux Klan members bombed a black church in Birmingham, Alabama on September 15, 1963, murdering four innocent young girls and injuring dozens of other members of the congregation. Many more people were injured in the aftermath, and two more were killed.

Addie Mae Collins, 14, Carole Robertson, 14, Cynthia Wesley, 14, and Denise McNair, 11, all good girls from good families, were murdered by Ku Klux Klan members because they were black. Denise McNair was known for having led other children in raising money for Muscular Dystrophy research.

One of her younger friends from school, Condoleezza Rice, would grow up to serve as National Security Advisor and US Secretary of State in the George W. Bush administration.

Reverend King, one of our nation's strongest true leaders by the early 1960s, again called for justice and an end to violence. His speeches played a pivotal role in the passage of the Civil Rights Act of 1964, partly because white Americans listened.

A Sudden and Violent Change

By late 1963, the man who lusted for power above all else had suffered in a power vacuum as VP for almost three years, after giving up his powerful position as Senate majority leader.

LBJ's fellow Texas Democrat, John Nance Garner, had given up his own powerful position as speaker of the House 28 years earlier in 1932, to serve as FDR's vice president. But Garner gave up his VP position, which he openly regarded as worthless, to challenge FDR for the presidency in 1940.

President Jack Kennedy called former VP "Cactus Jack" Garner on the morning of November 22, 1963, to wish him a happy 95th birthday. JFK was assassinated that afternoon while riding in a parade in Dallas, Texas. Ironically, JFK's murder freed LBJ from the powerless position that Garner had despised.

LBJ was sworn in as president two hours later. He had given up his position as Senate majority leader to serve as a powerless VP under JFK, a former fellow senator he strongly disliked. But he had been only a heartbeat away from the power of the presidency that he lusted after.

LBJ: Ready for Action

LBJ had prepared for this moment by burying his public image as leader of the Senate segregationists. With JFK gone, the last obstacle had been removed from his path to power.

Johnson inherited a position from which he could win a victory that was going to be won with or without him. The timing was perfect to help him fulfill his desire for power.

Quick passage of the Civil Rights Act would help him, so he drove it through Congress. He didn't have to persuade many Republicans, so he told Democrats in Congress that the best way they could honor JFK was by passing his Civil Rights Act (although Republican Senate Minority Leader Everett Dirksen played a major role in writing the final version).

He gave the Johnson "treatment" to Democrats whose votes would be important, and then gave impassioned public speeches. LBJ was well-prepared. He had a plan, and intended to win.

LBJ "courted" MLK and other black civil rights leaders, just as he had courted powerful segregationist Senate Democrats a few years earlier. He invited them to the White House for the Johnson treatment. But instead of pledging to enforce equal protection, he promised welfare, food stamps, and new rules of racial discrimination that appeared to favor them.

Three More KKK Murders

On the night of June 21, 1964, three college students working to register black voters against the will of Democrats, were arrested by police in Philadelphia, Mississippi on phony charges, and released later as the KKK waited.

Michael Schwerner, 24, James Chaney, 21, and Andrew Goodman, 20 were murdered that night, but their bodies weren't found until August. Their murders at the hands of KKK terrorists got extra attention because two of them were white. LBJ used their abduction to promote passage of the bill.

Victory for Freedom

The House passed the Civil Rights Act in February 1964. Senate Democrats blocked it, but LBJ didn't help them weaken it, as he had done to Eisenhower's civil rights bills.

Republican Senate Minority Leader Everett Dirksen helped force Senate Democrats to end their filibuster.

More than 80 percent of Republicans in Congress voted for passage of the Civil Rights Act, and its victory was so certain by then that some Democrats switched their votes at the last moment to be on the winning side. In the final tally, 65 percent of Democrats voted for it, too. Despite the overwhelming final margin of victory, the bill would never have become a law without the overwhelming support and actions of Republicans.

LBJ signed the Civil Rights Act on July 2, 1964, about ten months after Reverend King's speech about his dream.

King and the other brave men and women who put their safety and their lives on the line every day for civil rights would have prevailed eventually with or without LBJ, but he was instrumental in getting the bill passed before the 1964 election.

Goldwater vs. Johnson

The 1964 presidential election remains a powerful example of how US voters can be completely deceived about candidates by Mass Media Propaganda. That deception has contributed significantly to the destruction of US freedom in progress today.

While Lyndon Johnson led the segregationist Democrats in the Senate during the 1950s to crush and weaken every Republican attempt to establish equal protection for black Americans, Barry Goldwater established a strong track record of opposing segregation and racial discrimination.

Goldwater, a US Air Force Reserve officer who rose to Major General, desegregated the Arizona Air National Guard two years before Truman's 1948 order to finally undo Wilson's segregation of US Armed Forces. As a private business owner, Goldwater desegregated his family's department stores.

Goldwater was an active member of the NAACP and of the National Urban League, personally funding some of their early operations in Arizona. He also helped pay for a lawsuit that desegregated public schools in Arizona a year before the Supreme Court's 1954 *Brown* decision, in a case that apparently contributed to the Court's reasoning in *Brown*. [xxxii]

Goldwater was a friend and supporter of the American Indian tribes in Arizona. [xxxiii] He supported allowing gays to serve in US Armed Forces, reasoning that a man doesn't have to be straight to shoot straight.[xxxiv]

As a Republican senator, he desegregated the Senate cafeteria in 1953, after he learned that his black legislative assistant, Kathrine Maxwell, had been denied service. He voted for Eisenhower's Civil Rights Acts of 1957 and 1960, while LBJ was stalling their passage and weakening their provisions.

Although he was a strong supporter of civil rights, he voted against the Civil Rights Act of 1964 because he objected to two of its passages, primarily the one later used in establishing new rules of racial discrimination under Affirmative Action.

LBJ and Mass Media Propaganda (MMP) used Goldwater's vote against the Civil Rights Act of 1964 to paint him as a segregationist, while longtime segregationist LBJ was portrayed as the defender of rights for black Americans. Even MLK condemned him, although he knew Goldwater was not a racist.

Goldwater's vote against the Civil Rights Act of 1964 was a mistake. He strongly supported almost all of its provisions. His vote opposed most of what he stood for, harmed him, and helped MMP harm the Republican Party. He apparently recognized his mistake when he promised before the election to implement all of its provisions. But by then, no one was listening.

Even after his crushing 1964 election defeat, Goldwater's strict adherence to principle never wavered. In the 1970s, when a fellow Senator proposed releasing transcripts of tapes from wrongful FBI surveillance of MLK's alleged indiscretions, Goldwater immediately refused to help destroy MLK's reputation, and stopped the discussion dead in its tracks. [xxxv]

Goldwater was the true civil rights supporter in the 1964 election, and LBJ the segregationist, who had spent his days in the Senate "gutting anti-lynching laws and assuring Democrats that he would offer those 'uppity Negroes' just enough to quiet them down, not enough to make a difference." [xxxvi]

But the character assassination against Goldwater and cover-up of LBJs true record continues 50 years later in MMP and through public education / indoctrination.

These distortions deceived voters in 1964, and have contributed to the belief by millions of black and white Americans today in the fairy tale that Republicans oppose civil rights and that Democrats are champions of civil rights.

Many black Americans and whites who claim to support equal rights today still believe this myth.

Who Killed JFK?

LBJ obviously didn't pull the trigger, He was riding in the same parade and didn't appear to have gunpowder residue on his hands when he was sworn in so quickly after the assassination.

LBJ's close friend and neighbor in Washington, racist FBI Director J. Edgar Hoover, immediately began to investigate the assassination. A week later, LBJ created a commission of highly-regarded Americans to investigate the assassination and restore the confidence of any citizens who thought there might have been a conspiracy. After discussing the case with Hoover, LBJ hand-picked his commission members.

The Warren Commission members were not investigators, and had no means by which to actively investigate. They called hundreds of witnesses over several months, who mostly just supported Hoover's findings that Lee Harvey Oswald had acted alone, pulling the trigger of a bolt-action rifle three times in a few seconds with incredible accuracy, and that Jack Ruby had acted alone when he murdered Oswald two days later while Oswald was in police custody.

All the messy details were miraculously cleaned up. Oswald was dead. Ruby, who once claimed that others in very high positions were involved and that he had been forcibly injected with cancer cells, died of cancer while fighting his conviction.

Victory for LBJ

The Warren Commission ruled on September 24, 1964, that no one but Lee Harvey Oswald and Jack Ruby had anything to do with JFK's assassination or Oswald's murder.

Many Americans were skeptical, but the Warren Report and the Civil Rights Act helped LBJ win re-election by a landslide.

23

Another Victory for Freedom Diminished

Following in FDR's Footsteps: Maintaining the Crisis

LBJ had come into office during a crisis. He would keep the crisis going, make more people dependent on government, and cast himself as a champion of the people, just as FDR had done to make himself more powerful during the Great Depression.

When his government solutions prevented black Americans from overcoming racial discrimination and made their problems worse, he would call for more money and more power to solve the problems his policies caused, just as FDR had done.

LBJ prevented integration by promoting the Democratic core value of black racial inferiority. But this time he sold it to black Americans with a package of unrealistic expectations.

LBJ told black Americans that slavery and segregation had rendered them incapable of rising from poverty without his help and new rules of racial discrimination; that equality could not be achieved until government forced equal outcomes in all areas.

Turning Civil Rights Victory into Defeat

Black Americans were ready and willing to start overcoming the segregation to which Democrats had subjected them for 100 years. Equality under the law was what black men needed.

Frederick Douglass wrote about the black man 100 years earlier, "...All I ask is give him a chance to stand on his own legs! Let him alone!" [xxxvii]

The Civil Rights Act and the Voting Rights Act were the laws needed to enforce equal protection under the 14th and 15th Amendments. The president's job was to enforce those laws.

But LBJ didn't want to protect rights of black Americans. Equal protection was what Republicans wanted. LBJ wanted power, and to keep black people from voting for Republicans.

After a century of Republican anti-lynching and civil rights law proposals, Democrats were losing their ability to subjugate black Americans through segregation. So instead of enforcing equal protection, LBJ made up new rights to subjugate them under socialism. He would oblige government, as if it were a slave owner, to feed, clothe and house them, as he continued on FDR's path of selling all Americans on rights that don't exist.

Democrats had shifted their method of subjugation from slavery to segregation in 1865 when Republicans abolished slavery. LBJ shifted their method from segregation to socialism, in a way that kept black people mostly segregated.

War on Freedom

With Democratic majorities in Congress, Republicans couldn't stop LBJ. His "War on Poverty" and "Great Society" programs together constituted a powerful War on Freedom, expanding government control beyond levels FDR had reached.

Instead of the integrated schools and better jobs that equal protection would have produced, LBJ and Democrats "paid off" black Americans with welfare and food stamp programs that broke up black families, kept them poor, encouraged crime, and make them dependent on the federal government.

When the Civil Rights Act of 1964 passed, some black men were already successful as doctors, lawyers, in other professions, and in sports and entertainment, where personal ability was easy to measure and segregation was already breaking down.

Defeat of the Democratic Jim Crow segregation laws opened opportunities, but black Americans who fell into the trap of food stamps, welfare, and federal housing were mostly segregated as a permanent underclass on the modern Democratic plantation.

Welfare, Crime, and Destruction of Families

Paying a person for not working takes away his incentive to work. When you pay him just enough to keep him poor but take it away if he works, he is unlikely to find a job. But poor doesn't mean stupid or lazy. Not working leaves time to make money from unreported, untaxed activities, including crime.

Paying women to have children with no father present makes a father less important and his presence financially undesirable. Almost 75 percent[xxxviii] of black children today are born to single mothers, compared to 25 percent in 1960. Welfare destroys families and deprives children of needed parental supervision.

The welfare state is hard to escape. After a few years or a few generations, this way of life seems impossible to escape.

Economist Thomas Sowell, a black American who lived through the 1960s, wrote, "The black family survived centuries of slavery and generations of Jim Crow, but it disintegrated in the wake of the liberals' expansion of the welfare state." [xxxix]

Federal Housing

Starting in 1965, the Department of Housing and Urban Development (HUD) paid cities to build housing for the black urban underclass Democrats were developing.

Baltimore, the scene of recent riots, was one of those cities. The projects quickly became breeding grounds for crime, where black people were the chief victims and the chief perpetrators, and criminals were the only ones who felt safe.

HUD and Democratic city councils "solved" the crime problem by increasing Section 8 housing, which didn't decrease crime, but expanded its territory.

HUD would later destabilize other neighborhoods, increase foreclosures, and decrease property values through subsidized mortgages for low-income buyers who couldn't make payments.

Trillions of dollars have been spent to keep millions of black Americans from escaping today's Democratic urban plantations, while the poverty rate has remained largely unchanged.

But Democratic politicians claim the only solution is more spending to solve the problems their spending has caused. The only problem they want to solve is how to maintain control.

Malcolm X Assassination

Malcolm X was a prominent leader of the Nation of Islam, widely suspected to have been heavily infiltrated by FBI operatives under racist Director Hoover. He received death threats after leaving the Nation of Islam in 1964, and he was portrayed by MMP as a trouble-maker who demanded too much. But Malcolm X had a few things right.

Malcolm X spoke the truth, exposing LBJ as a segregationist and Democrats as racists.

Malcolm X

"(When) you are dumb enough to walk around continuing to identify yourself with that party, you're not only a chump, but you're a traitor to your race."

You, today, are in the hands of a government of segregationists, racists, white supremacists, who belong to the Democratic Party..."

"I say it, I say it again. You've got a president who is nothing but a southern segregationist."

"And the first thing the cracker does when he comes in power, he takes all the Negro leaders and invites them for coffee to show that he's all right. And these Uncle Toms can't pass up the coffee. They come away from the coffee table telling you and me that this man is all right. No, I say, you've been misled. You've been had. You've been took." [xl]

A few days after his speech, Malcolm X was murdered by three Nation of Islam members on February 21, 1965, during the early stages of LBJ's "War on Poverty" and "Great Society."

Democratically Delayed Voting Rights and Selma

LBJ proposed and promoted the Voting Rights Act of 1965, which would likely not have been needed if he hadn't weakened Eisenhower's Civil Rights Acts just a few years earlier, when he was Senate Democratic Majority Leader.

Civil rights activists organized peaceful marches for voting rights in Alabama, including three marches from Selma to Montgomery, which were met with violent attacks by the KKK and police under the control of Democratic public officials.

The injuries, deaths, and national spectacle of Selma might have been avoided altogether if LBJ and fellow Democrats had not weakened Eisenhower's bills in 1957 and 1960.

The 1965 Voting Rights Act was overwhelmingly supported by Republicans, who had led that fight for years. But it took the carnage caused by Democrats in Selma for a strong voting rights law to finally receive majority support from Democrats.

"Reverse Discrimination"

Affirmative Action's new rules of racial discrimination made race a part of decisions on corporate hiring and promotions and on college admissions. Instead of equal opportunity, it attempted to impose an unrealistic socialist vision of equal outcome.

Equal protection would have brought integration and justice, but this new inequality just changed the rules of segregation.

Why It Was Accepted

After the long struggle for civil rights, many believed that "more" than equality was temporarily needed. But righting one wrong by imposing another doesn't make anything right.

Black Americans had another reason to buy into this idea. An abused person wants to believe that his or her abuser has changed. That's why abused family members often refuse to file charges after an abuser simply makes a promise to change.

Former slaves Frederick Douglass [xli] and John R. Lynch both expressed this feeling [xlii] about former slave owners in their writing. Many wanted to believe that the party of slavery and segregation had changed, but the only things Democrats changed were the methods they used to control black people.

Many accepted the flawed logic that "reverse discrimination" would somehow make up for what Democrats had done to black Americans. But government cannot right a wrong previously committed against individuals of one group by committing a similar wrong against random other individuals.

LBJ's actions thwarted MLK's dream of judging each other by the content of our character, and guaranteed that judgment by the color of our skin would continue.

Many accepted the new Democratic policies of racial discrimination, assuming they would be temporary—the same mistake Americans made in allowing slavery to continue when the Constitution was ratified in 1788, believing that it would end shortly after Congress could ban the slave trade in 1808.

But there was nothing temporary about these policies. They are well established, just as segregation and racial discrimination against black Americans were under Democratic Jim Crow laws.

Turning the Tables

Republicans ended slavery, ratified the 13th, 14th, and 15th Amendments, opposed segregation and lynching, led the way to school desegregation, and overwhelmingly supported the Civil Rights and Voting Rights Acts. And many white Republicans were among the victims of KKK lynchings and terrorism.

But when Republicans refused to support new rules of racial discrimination, Mass Media painted Republicans as racists who opposed civil rights, and Democrats as champions of the cause. The truth didn't matter to them, and it hasn't mattered since.

Mass Media Propaganda has told us many stories to explain away this total subversion of truth, and many believe their fairy tale that the party of slavery and segregation suddenly and magically changed to become the champions of equal rights.

Norman Whitfield and Barrett Strong may not have had LBJ and Democrats in mind when they wrote their hit song "Smiling Faces Sometimes (tell lies)," by the Undisputed Truth, but it fits.

Democrats Re-establish Ownership

LBJ found a way for Democrats to own 90 percent of the voting power of black Americans, after they had owned three-fifths (60 percent) of their voting power during slavery, and suppressed their votes during segregation.

The man who had found more votes to win after his Senate election defeat, [xliii] led Democrats to extend the racial injustice caused by slavery and segregation after both were defeated.

Indoctrination and Control

Democrats then used federal funds to take greater control over elementary and secondary schools and higher education.

LBJ signed legislation to reorganize the Public Broadcasting Service (PBS) and National Public Radio (NPR), which produce smooth-spoken propaganda promoting more federal control to children and unsuspecting adults today.

To make local governments directly dependent, Democrats expanded funding for public works, police departments, and art.

Like FDR before him, LBJ was willing to try almost anything that involved more federal control.

Federal Control of Medical Care

LBJ's Medicare and a Social Security tax increase roughly doubled the payroll taxes workers and employers paid and started the upward spiral in medical costs for all Americans.

Doctors were forced to submit more paperwork, wait longer to be paid, and accept less for services to covered patients, which forced them to raise rates for everyone to just stay even.

Vietnam War and the Draft

World War II helped FDR win re-election to his third and fourth terms, but LBJ's conduct of the Vietnam War ruined his plans for re-election in 1968, which had once seemed certain.

US military forces were clearly superior, and won every major battle. But political limits that LBJ and Congress placed on their commanders kept US troops from winning the war.

LBJ couldn't withdraw from the war and be a seen as a loser, so he kept drafting American boys and sending them to fight a war that he had no plan to win, while protests mounted.

Ironically, LBJ's domestic policies on taxes, education, and federal control followed steps from the Communist Manifesto, as he sent troops to Vietnam to fight the spread of communism.

LBJ's Power Failure

LBJ failed to achieve the power his mentor enjoyed, but he took FDR's destruction of constitutional limits to a new level, even while his party was divided. Anti-war activists, union bosses, segregationists, civil rights advocates, and socialists all had conflicts with each other and with LBJ.

MLK broke publicly with LBJ by speaking in opposition to his conduct of the war in Vietnam on April 4, 1967.

Incumbent presidents had seldom been seriously challenged in primaries, but anti-war Senator Eugene McCarthy drew 42 percent of the New Hampshire Democratic Primary vote on March 12, 1968.

Robert F. Kennedy (RFK) had resigned as Attorney General to win a Senate seat after LBJ replaced his brother as president. But now seeing LBJ as vulnerable, RFK entered the presidential primary race on March 16.

LBJ couldn't allow himself to be defeated for the nomination by McCarthy or by RFK, whose brother had defeated him in 1960, delaying his rise to the presidency. So he shocked many by abandoning his own candidacy for re-election on March 31.

MLK Assassination

On April 4, 1968, a few days after LBJ withdrew, Reverend Martin Luther King, Jr. was assassinated, one year after his first speech opposing LBJ on the War in Vietnam. An escaped convict who later claimed to have been set up was convicted of acting alone, despite unproven allegations of FBI involvement.

On April 27, LBJ's Vice President Hubert Humphrey entered the primary race, before the next assassination.

RFK Assassination

On June 5, Robert F. Kennedy was assassinated hours after winning the California Democratic Primary, and died the next morning, on June 6, 1968. His murderer, a 24-year-old Palestinian, also convicted of acting alone, complained that RFK had supported Israel after the six day war in 1967. He displayed bizarre behavior during his trial and later claimed to have no memory of his crime, confession, or trial.

Unrelated Previous Assassinations

JFK was assassinated on November 22, 1963. LBJ's hand-picked Warren Commission cleared LBJ quickly, validating the investigation by his friend, racist FBI Director J. Edgar Hoover.

After Malcolm X was suddenly silenced on February 21, 1965, [xliv] no strong black leader stood up publicly against LBJ again until MLK did on April 4, 1967, one year before he died.

JFK, Malcolm X, MLK, and RFK were all inconvenient to LBJ when they were murdered. Their alleged assassins were caught, isolated, and quickly "proven" guilty or silenced.

None, including the three who murdered Malcolm X, was found to be part of any conspiracy.

RFK seemed the least inconvenient, but one might wonder what he knew about his brother's murder that could have been proven with RFK in full control of the executive branch.

Gun Control

LBJ and Democrats in Congress reacted to the assassinations by blaming the guns. So to punish the guns, they limited the rights of citizens by passing the Gun Control Act of 1968.

24

One-Party Domination

Democratic National Convention and Chaos

When LBJ stepped aside in 1968, the Democratic Party was in chaos and had the nation in a state of upheaval. Race riots followed the murder of Reverend King in April. Anti-war protests led to violent clashes with Chicago police during the Democratic National Convention in August.

Anti-US military Democrats, including now-Secretary of State John Kerry and movie star "Hanoi Jane" Fonda, focused personal attacks on US soldiers and openly supported communist US enemies in North Vietnam.

The Weather Underground, a terrorist group led by now-President Obama's friend Bill Ayers, bombed federal buildings.

Other Democrats who opposed US principles of freedom and limited government adopted Saul Alinsky's methods, aiming to overthrow the US government and civilized society. One of Alinsky's disciples who cultivated a personal relationship with him was Hillary Rodham, now known as Hillary Clinton.

LBJ's power failed him in 1968, but strengthened the special interest groups of Democrats seeking control. By the time he left office, Democrats had defeated most Constitutional limits that protected our freedom, and were working from within to turn US government into the monster our founders had tried to prevent.

Democratic Diversity Achieved

Democrats achieved diversity as segregationists who owned the votes of black Americans anyway, union bosses, former civil rights leaders LBJ had converted, and anti-US military anarchists including members of the news media and the Hollywood elite. They overlapped, but had different, often conflicting goals.

They all wanted to use government force to control others, and accepted the founding Democratic core value of black racial inferiority, apparently including the civil rights leaders who had traded their goal of equality for socialist promises by Democrats.

The Rise of Mass Media Propaganda to Replace the KKK

Democrats couldn't state all their mutually exclusive goals honestly and maintain an alliance strong enough to control us.

The national news media proved its propaganda could make Americans believe almost anything, by falsely painting the party of slavery and segregation as champions of civil rights, while painting Republicans as racists in public perception.

Cross and church burnings, lynchings, rapes, beatings, and other KKK methods were becoming less effective, so MMP took control to replace the KKK as the party's enforcement arm.

Sticking Together with a Coordinated Message

To avoid conflicts, MMP ignored what Democrats stood for, but reported news from their many fantasy-based perspectives.

They have led many to believe that the federal government has a duty to solve every problem, union bosses always fight for all workers, the use of military force is always wrong, the job of government is to redistribute wealth, and guns cause violence.

MMP Speech Police

MMP suppresses free speech to protect Democrats. No one can use words that offend them. Above all, no one can publicly mention the Democratic core value of black racial inferiority.

Anyone who violates their "politically correct" speech rules will be attacked repeatedly until he apologizes or resigns from his public position and his allies condemn his words.

LBJ's claim that black Americans are incapable of anything without government help is never stated but always implied. MMP never admits that all the slave owners and segregationists were Democrats, and tries to imply that they were Republicans. Welcome to their version of *Alice in Wonderland!*

Speech Police in Academia

Universities indoctrinate students into the same fantasies, but go a step further by blatantly silencing free speech on campus.

One Party Dominance of the Two Party System

Democrats have dominated Congress for over 80 years, and have controlled government even when they haven't held all the cards, through their monstrous bureaucracy that continues to grow, spend, regulate, and increase dependence on government.

Their control has sometimes been facilitated by "moderate" Republicans who compromise away our freedom.

National Defense and Security

National defense is the most basic duty of our federal government, and the main justification for its existence. But Democrats consistently weaken our national defense, as they focus their efforts on controlling Americans.

Republicans have not held enough power for long enough to refocus government on consistently protecting our freedom.

Administrative Law

The federal administrative bureaucracy has taken over most legislative functions. When Congress passes laws, bureaucrats not only write the rules, but enforce them. They effectively act as legislators, prosecutors, judges, and juries, which defeats the Constitutional safeguard of three branches.

Since their focus is on controlling us, Democrats are drawn to federal jobs. They've formed unions and enacted rules to help them remain in those positions, dominating the bureaucracy even when a Republican president is in office.

Following Marx's Plan

With help from compromising Republicans, Democrats follow steps from the Communist Manifesto: attacking families and religious freedom, establishing educational indoctrination almost from birth, and imposing graduated taxes.

They use forfeiture laws to seize property from citizens not even charged with crimes. They've centralized communications, credit, and transportation under control of the state, and control farms and factories as if government owns them. They exercise control over private companies, and threaten to seize more.

25

The Nixon through Clinton Years

Nixon / Ford

After the 1968 election, strong Democratic majorities, including many segregationists, returned to Congress. Anti-war upheaval continued.

George Wallace, as a segregationist third party candidate, split the Democratic vote with Hubert Humphrey, so Republican Richard Nixon was elected 37th US president. After Wallace ran again in 1972, segregationists returned to their Democratic roots.

Democrats still promote a fantasy that Nixon converted all the segregationist Democrats to the Republican Party with his "Southern Strategy," because he promoted law and order at a time when Democrats had the country in a state of upheaval. But Nixon won the election only because so many Democrats voted for Wallace. Many of the same hard-core segregationist Democrats kept getting re-elected to Congress.

Assassinations of people inconvenient to LBJ stopped.

Nixon, who had helped Eisenhower promote the Civil Rights Acts of 1957 and 1960, racially integrated schools, reduced waste in federal grants, and re-directed funds back to the States.

But he also imposed temporary wage and price controls, a national speed limit, ended convertibility of US currency to gold, and helped Democrats create the Environmental Protection Agency (EPA), which has become a repressive monster.

Nixon established trade with the Peoples Republic of China (PRC), effectively a communist slave nation, in 1972. He didn't establish full diplomatic relations because they demanded the US end diplomatic relations with the free Republic of China (ROC) on Taiwan, a strong and faithful US ally, and terminate the 1954 US mutual defense treaty with the ROC.

Under Nixon, US forces trained the South Vietnamese military to take over the fighting in Vietnam. With the support of Congress, he ended the military draft and signed a treaty to withdraw US troops from Vietnam in January 1973, promising support for South Vietnam if North Vietnam violated the treaty.

After his wrongful cover-up allowed Democrats and MMP to blow the relatively minor Watergate scandal into a national crisis, Nixon resigned in August 1974.

Republican VP Gerald Ford succeeded him as 38th president. Ford ended the temporary wage and price controls, but federal regulations and spending continued to increase.

North Vietnam attacked two years after US withdrawal, but the Democratic Congress refused to fulfill our country's promise to help, even with military supplies only, persuading communists that the US was weak. South Vietnam fell in 1975.

US troops under Ford stood up to attacks in Cambodia and Korea, but after US failure to help South Vietnam, a communist genocide in Cambodia and Southeast Asia claimed a million plus lives with help from North Vietnam, the PRC, and the USSR.

Democratic Dominance and Carter's Malaise

Democrat Jimmy Carter took office as 39th US president in 1977 with a Democratic Congress. They expanded Energy and Education to cabinet-level and increased EPA regulation, which helped increase unemployment and federal spending.

Carter promoted affirmative action (racial discrimination), signed a civil service bill that made federal bureaucrats less responsive to citizens, and a housing bill that helped lead to the later mortgage loan crisis. Carter used "malaise" to describe the economy he left with inflation and interest rates in double-digits.

But malaise was too mild a word to describe his national defense failures. He started by cancelling military pay raises, and then gave away the Panama Canal.

Carter deluded himself that he could negotiate peace in the Middle East while Palestinian terrorists continued shooting missiles and dedicating their lives to destroying Israel.

While Congress was on Christmas recess in 1978, Carter established full diplomatic relations with the communist PRC, bowing to their demand that he sever relations with the free Republic of China, and end our 1954 Mutual Defense Treaty with the ROC, which was why Nixon had not established full relations. Trade could have continued without that step.

Carter's incompetent handling of the Iranian Hostage Crisis allowed Muslim terrorists to hold 52 Americans hostage in the US Embassy in Iran for 444 days, and persuaded our enemies that US national defense was weak and vulnerable.

Reagan Restoration and Prosperity

Republican Ronald Reagan won the 1980 election in a landslide and took office in 1981 as 40th US president, with a Democratic House and a Republican Senate. He was shot ten weeks later, but survived the assassination attempt.

His election prompted the Muslim terrorist regime in Iran to release the American hostages who had been held for 444 days. Reagan recognized that his first responsibility was US security, and he set out to restore the strength of our national defense.

Reagan persuaded Congress to cut taxes and reduce business overregulation. The economy grew, unemployment and Carter's double digit interest and inflation rates fell. Individual incomes rose, and income tax revenues rose after the rate decrease.

Reagan was committed to enforcing civil rights, and black Americans shared in the prosperity. Black unemployment dropped, incomes of black-owned businesses increased, the black middle class grew, and black household incomes rose. [xlv]

He trimmed the bureaucracy by about 5 percent, but Congress increased spending on education, social services, and other programs, causing the deficit and national debt to grow despite the increased tax revenue.

Reagan's brief use of US military strength restored order in Grenada in 1983. His one-day 1986 bombing of military targets in Libya, including Muammar Gaddafi's house, reduced the dictator's support for anti-western terrorist attacks.

107

The US helped Iraq in their 1980-1988 war with Iran. But in 1986, Reagan administration officials apparently sold weapons to Iran, funneling profits to support the "Contras" in their fight against communists who then controlled Nicaragua, after Congress had cut off funds to them. The Iran-Contra Affair was halted, and Reagan apologized for his administration's actions.

Reagan's military build-up and his nuclear missile defense plan, ridiculed in Mass Media Propaganda as a "Star Wars" fantasy, helped bring down the Berlin Wall, which communists had built to keep East Germans from escaping to freedom, and was instrumental in the later collapse of the Soviet Union.

Ronald Reagan

Bush 41 and the Democratic Congress

Republican George H.W. Bush, now often called Bush 41, followed Reagan in 1989 as 41st president.

Failing to follow Reagan's example, Bush and a Democratic Congress increased spending, regulation, and the bureaucracy. Two new laws forced banks to increase high-risk housing loans, which would contribute to the later mortgage loan crisis.

They passed affirmative action quotas and the Americans with Disabilities Act (ADA), and increased the minimum wage, which slowed the economy and increased unemployment. The cost of the flood of new regulations was overly burdensome.

But like Reagan, Bush 41 recognized his responsibility for national defense and fulfilled it well.

Iraqi dictator Saddam Hussein, who had used torture, rape, murder, mutilation, and chemical weapons against his own people, was heavily in debt to his smaller neighbor Kuwait, a strategic US ally and US oil supplier that had helped Iraq.

When Kuwait declined to forgive Iraq's war debt, Saddam Hussein invaded Kuwait in August 1990. His army raped and murdered civilians as they defeated Kuwait's military, occupied the country, and took control of their oil wells.

Bush assembled and led a coalition of 30 countries including Saudi Arabia, the UK and Egypt, and drove Saddam Hussein's Iraqi Army out of Kuwait in six weeks during early 1991.

Bush allowed Saddam Hussein to remain in power after he agreed by treaty to destroy all his weapons of mass destruction and to allow UN inspectors to continuously verify compliance. But Bush's treaty went completely unenforced by Bill Clinton.

After his promise not to raise taxes, Bush compromised with Democrats in Congress and signed their tax increase, apparently hoping to avoid further increasing the national debt.

Despite Bush's superior defense leadership in the Persian Gulf War, regulations, taxes, and spending increased almost as if a Democrat had been in office. Bill Clinton won election with 43 percent of the popular vote when Democrat Ross Perot took 19 percent as a fiscally conservative third party candidate.

The Clinton White House

Democrat Bill Clinton took office as 42nd US president in 1993, and made many Americans regret their votes for Perot.

When foreign Muslim terrorists bombed the World Trade Center in New York a month after his inauguration, Clinton treated their foreign aggression as if it were a domestic crime.

But when an American religious fanatic refused to surrender to police at a Waco, Texas ranch a few weeks later, Clinton claimed federal jurisdiction and launched military-style attacks that killed 80 religious sect members and four federal agents.

Clinton and Democrats in Congress made voter fraud easier and increased consumer prices, taxes, and regulations, including gun control. After two years, voters elected the first Republican House majority in 40 years and a Republican Senate majority.

Republicans negotiated with him to fulfill their "Contract with America," since they couldn't override a veto. He signed their bills to reduce the rapid growth of federal spending, regulations, and welfare. Clinton signed their balanced budget and took credit for balancing it.

Clinton and wife Hillary claimed she was his co-president, but she was more a co-conspirator in their house of scandals. They were investigated for suspicious land deals she had made in Arkansas. When her former law partner was found shot to death after reportedly admitting her unethical actions, she seized his office files and hid them from investigators in the White House for long enough to remove any incriminating documents.

Hillary proposed a plan to take ownership interest in our bodies through federal control over health care, similar to the plan she later helped Obama, Reid, and Pelosi impose.

When Bill was accused of sexual crimes and abuse against women including a White House intern, Hillary fought back with denials and character assassinations. He reportedly had a history of demanding sex from women for jobs and favors, but he and Hillary had silenced women who accused him of rape and sexual imposition by personally attacking the alleged victims.

While Clinton and Democratic MMP accused Republicans who opposed abortion of a "war on women," Bill and Hillary conducted a real war on the women who were his victims.

Clinton failed to enforce the US treaty with Iraq, and gave up on weapons inspections in 1998. Just before the House voted to impeach him, he bombed Baghdad, reportedly destroying an aspirin factory to distract attention from his personal misconduct.

Killing Iraqi civilians didn't seem to bother Saddam Hussein, who had killed so many himself, and Muslim leaders customarily use women and children as "human shields."

Clinton was impeached for perjury and obstruction of justice, but MMP made Americans believe it was about marital infidelity. Some called Hillary a victim, and others blamed her.

After the Senate failed to remove him from office, he agreed to a five year suspension of his Arkansas law license and a $90,000 fine for perjury in one of his sex abuse cases.

Clinton's weak response to the World Trade Center bombing, failure to enforce the treaty with Iraq, and haphazard use of military force elsewhere persuaded terrorist leader Osama bin Laden and Iraqi dictator Saddam Hussein that US national defense was weak and vulnerable. The results of his defense failures would soon visit us in New York and Washington.

26

Who Owns Us?

Freedom vs. Ownership

A slave is a person compelled against his will to serve the wants and needs of another. A slave can't keep money he earns, but his owner provides whatever food, clothing, housing, and medical care the owner deems necessary.

A free man owns his life, his time and effort, and the money he earns from his work, but must pay for his own personal needs.

Taxes are necessary to pay for the cost of a government that protects our freedom. Our founders established that government through the US Constitution, defining the duties for which it could tax us and the ways in which we could be taxed.

Providing for everyone's needs may sound great, but using government force to take from some and give to others compels us to serve the wants and needs of others against our will.

Where does unlawful taking from us cross that line?

Our founders drew the line clearly.   The government created by the US Constitution didn't promise to provide for our needs, but to protect our freedom and natural rights.

An overwhelming majority of the people agreed to the US Constitution, including the provision that it could be changed only by an Amendment process requiring an overwhelming majority of citizens and our elected leaders to approve changes.

Ownership by Government

Democrats, with the help of compromising Republicans over the last 100 years, have broken those limits. Through taxes, the government designed to protect us is stealing our freedom.

How Much of Our Lives and Liberty Belong to Government?

Federal, state, and local governments take about half of everything we earn through taxes, and take more through regulation. Government hides the taxes it takes from our pay by taking them before we receive "our share" of what we earn, and obscures the rest by collecting it directly from our employers.

We pay 15.3 percent of our wages for Social Security and Medicare, but only half of it is shown on our pay stubs, because employers must pay the other half directly. But it's all money we earn, that our employers must pay for our work.

So if you're adding up what's actually taken from your pay, add the hidden 7.65 percent paid directly by your employer for Social Security and Medicare taxes to the 25 to 35 percent or more shown on your pay stub for federal, state, and local taxes.

Also add unemployment, worker's compensation, and other taxes your employer pays for your work, which can be 3 to 5 percent or more. All of it is money your employer must pay for your labor, and brings the total to around 35 to 50 percent of what you earn. But that's just part of what we pay.

A Few of the Other Taxes

Most products we buy are taxed at least once or twice before they reach us, and some are taxed many times. We pay those taxes, too, in the price we pay for the product.

Truckers pay taxes on gasoline and tires, and pay tolls to deliver goods to us. We pay those taxes, too, within the price. When politicians tell us they're taxing a business instead of us, they're lying. We pay all those taxes, and the resulting higher sales taxes, which vary by State.

We all pay property taxes. If you rent, you may think you don't, but you do. The tax is in your rent. Property taxes paid by grocers, gas stations, and other retailers are in the cost of what we buy, too. And we pay taxes on cell phones, home phones, cable television, and almost every other service we use.

Add it all up, and we pay about half or more than half of what we earn in taxes, before counting the costs of regulations by which the EPA and other agencies raise the cost of everything we buy. Does that make us slaves, or half-slaves?

113

Marx believed that all money and property rightfully belong to the people, meaning the government. We're about halfway there. Should we let them take it all, or just a bit less than that?

Still Not Enough

Our founders revolted against oppressive taxes and control, and created a government to protect freedom. But it's become more oppressive than the government they revolted against.

Yet all the taxes we pay are not nearly enough to support the illegitimate spending of our leaders, who always want more.

Our federal government spends billions on ideas that sound good to some of us, and spends billions more on a bureaucracy to control us, with almost no limits.

Many federal workers are good employees, but of roughly two million, about half are members of powerful unions that protect incompetent and ineffective employees. Their union bosses are so powerful that they can threaten retaliation against members of Congress who even try to reduce the workforce.

And our taxes pay the exorbitant costs of federal labor regulations and "prevailing wages" on government projects, to pay off the union bosses who pay off the Democrats.

But at a time when our President is making the world more dangerous, we're told we must cut back on military strength.

When an Interstate Highway bridge between States needs to be replaced, we're told to replace it ourselves and charge tolls.

Democrats want to take even more from us. Republicans object, but a few will usually compromise and settle for taking just a little less than the dominant Democrats demand.

Now they're stealing from our children and grandchildren by adding to a $19 trillion debt we can never repay, which will be left for them to pay. Is this taxation without representation, or a new way for our children to be born into slavery?

27

The Massive Lie of Social Security

Social Security: A Disastrous Fairy Tale Now Collapsing

US Presidents and Members of Congress have been lying to us about Social Security since 1936. But despite their repeated assurances, the facts should not make anyone feel secure.

First, there's no money in the Social Security retirement fund to pay benefits, because there is no fund. Social Security accounts exist only on paper and electronic spreadsheets.

Second, there was no constitutional authority to establish Social Security. Social Security is a tax, sold to Americans with a promise to pay retirement benefits, but the Supreme Court has ruled twice that our federal government is not legally obliged to make any of the promised payments.

Third, Social Security is not just close to bankruptcy. It has been effectively bankrupt for years. Every payment depends on borrowed money and future tax collections.

The Original Promises of Social Security

Americans were sold on Social Security as a retirement pension fund. But one of its original goals was to reduce the work force and open jobs for younger workers to replace the jobs FDR's New Deal was destroying during the Great Depression, by giving older workers an incentive to retire. It boiled down to just another socialist welfare program. [xlvi]

Social Security promised to set up a separate retirement account for each person who paid the "contributions," and that benefit checks would come to them as a right.

The maximum cost would never exceed $180 per year per taxpayer ($90 from the worker, and $90 from the employer). The promise continued, that you and your employer will each pay three cents on each dollar you earn, up to $3,000 a year....That is the most you will ever pay.

Americans were also promised that social security account numbers would not be used for identification.

No Retirement Fund, Just a Tax and a Promise

There is no Social Security Retirement Fund, except on paper. The tax payments go into the general fund. The Social Security "lockbox" that politicians talk about is an accounting spreadsheet backed only by their IOUs, because they've stolen all the money every year to spend on whatever they think will get them re-elected. The accounts exist only on paper and electronic spreadsheets, with no actual money to back them.

The tax originally skimmed two percent, gradually rising to six percent, from the pay of each worker. Including a Medicare tax that was added later, the tax now takes 15.3 percent of the first $118,500 that each American earns annually, whether you make $1,000 or $118,500, and even more if you make more.

If Social Security had been set up as a retirement fund within the rules Congress requires of legitimate retirement funds, there would be real funds, and the benefits retirees receive from it would be much higher, regardless of stock market fluctuations. But our accounts are not funds; just promises to pay.

Illegitimate and Unconstitutional

The US government had no authority under the Constitution to create Social Security or any other welfare program, despite the absurd ruling the Supreme Court made in the 1936 *Butler* case that it gave Congress power to do anything they deemed to be for the general welfare of all citizens. If that were true, there would have been no reason to enumerate the duties and powers granted to Congress.

Despite the *Butler* ruling, the Supreme Court probably would have overruled the Social Security Act if their 1937 decision had not been made under the duress of intimidation by FDR, who was using the Depression to rule almost as a dictator. The US

Constitution granted only limited powers, and the power to control Americans through Social Security was not among them.

That was clearly understood for 148 years, from 1788 to 1936, and the Supreme Court has no legitimate power to amend the Constitution through its rulings.

Under No Obligation to Pay

Americans have been told many times that benefit checks would come to us as a right, but the Supreme Court ruled in *Helvering v. Davis* in 1937 and again in *Flemming v. Nestor* in 1960 that Americans have no legal right to receive Social Security retirement benefits.

The Court noted that Social Security taxes are paid into the Treasury like other Internal Revenue taxes with no earmarks whatsoever, and that any right of taxpayers to receive benefit payments would rob the federal government of "flexibility."

Despite these Supreme Court rulings and the fact that the system is clearly unconstitutional, the victims of this massive fraud who have paid taxes into a fictional retirement fund for 80 years absolutely do have a legitimate claim. We can't let the federal government ignore its obligations, but we can't let this disaster continue as is, to destroy our freedom and our future.

The System is Bankrupt

The US government is borrowing, printing, and spending many billions of dollars more than it takes in each year and has accumulated a $19 trillion national debt. That's a personal debt of over $60 thousand for each American man, woman, and child. Our nation and our Social Security are effectively bankrupt.

Relatively few Americans lived past age 65 in 1936, but that has changed. In 1950, there were 16 workers paying Social Security taxes for each retiree receiving payments. Today, there are fewer than 3, and that number is shrinking.

Social Security promises to pay benefits from taxes the federal government will take by force of law from us, our children, and grandchildren--until it bankrupts our children and grandchildren and wipes out their ability to pay. With our government now borrowing about 40 percent of everything it spends, that day has arrived. But we're told repeatedly that it's 40, 30, 20, or 18 years away.

Some Republicans have compared Social Security to a Ponzi scheme, but it's actually worse. Fraudulent Ponzi schemes hurt their victims, but are at least recognized as illegal. The number of victims is limited, as the schemes eventually run dry and collapse after new victims cease to be fooled.

Many Americans have ceased to be fooled by this one, but our government plans to make our children and grandchildren keep paying more and more forever. If we don't deal with this problem now, the collapse of Social Security, national defense, and our whole government will harm all of us.

Why Hasn't Social Security Been Repaired?

This fraud can't continue indefinitely. The problem has been building for a long time, but our President and members of Congress have made it worse, and placed benefit payments to all current and future recipients in danger.

A few Republicans have warned over the last 30 years that the system is unsustainable without changes, but they've been shouted down by Democratic leaders who accuse them of trying to steal retirement benefits from people who have paid the taxes all their lives. Democratic Mass Media Propaganda (MMP) smears anyone who admits the truth or proposes a solution.

Democrats created this illegitimate system. Social Security and their other socialist programs have brought the whole federal government to the point of collapse.

Democrats won't fix it because they don't want government to protect our freedom. Democrats want control. Republicans have backed off because they never have the votes to fix it, and many are afraid to try. A collapse, a drastic change, or both are not only inevitable, but already beginning. Democratic MMP will blame this disaster on whoever tries to lessen its impact.

28

An Inconvenient and Destructive Hoax

An Early American Destructive Hoax

During the 1600s in Salem, Massachusetts, the "moral leaders" of the community blamed every troubling phenomenon that was hard to explain on witchcraft. They used rumors, lies, and fabricated evidence to frighten people and make them feel threatened, to justify putting the women they accused of being witches to death, to prove whether or not they were guilty.

Like Witchcraft Trials All Over Again

Today, Democrats claim moral leadership and blame every troubling natural phenomenon on man-made global warming or climate change. They use rumors, lies, and fabricated evidence to frighten people and make us feel threatened, to justify putting our freedom and prosperity to death, to prove whether or not we are guilty of this modern substitute for witchcraft.

They claim scientific proof that we, not God or nature, control the earth's climate, and that our lives cause an imminent threat to the earth's survival.

Science and Junk Science

Dramatic natural changes have been taking place on earth for millions of years. Temperatures and sea levels have been rising and falling since long before humans existed. Plates have shifted. Land masses have risen from the sea and disappeared below it. The tsunami in Japan and a new island that rose from the Red Sea a few years ago remind us that natural change is still occurring. But socialists and their "scientists" blame it on us.

The earth has experienced warming and cooling cycles for millions of years. Some run 25-30 years, others much longer.

The collapse of an Antarctic ice sheet 14,000 years ago is said to have caused a sudden world-wide rise in sea level of 46-60 feet. Humans obviously didn't cause that, but a similar event today would be even more catastrophic than many predictions by promoters of man-made climate change hysteria.

The Ice Age was real. Much of our country was covered by a thick glacier 10,000 years ago, and some of our largest rivers were created by its melting. What caused the ice that blanketed North America to melt and disappear? Our factories, cars and SUVs didn't exist then.

Mass Media Propaganda tells us repeatedly that "the science is settled," and scientists have proven beyond a doubt that man-made pollution from the US is the cause of global warming. But some noteworthy scientists disagree. [xlvii]

Fabrications and flaws in their evidence have been exposed, but they just shrug them off and persist. Junk science proof is what you get when you set an agenda, then pay scientists to produce data to support it. If we pay their "scientists" enough federal tax dollars, they can prove almost anything.

Are we warming or cooling? It doesn't matter to promoters of this hoax. Their purpose is to scare us. They warned us 40 years ago of impending doom from global cooling, but then it became global warming. Facts don't matter to them as long as their "facts" scare us.

The Absurdity of the Hoax

It would be absurd to argue that there has been no global warming or cooling, and equally absurd to argue that man-made pollution is harmless. There has been plenty of warming and cooling, and we should avoid polluting our air and water.

But to claim that scientists have proven beyond reasonable doubt that US man-made pollution is the cause of harmful global warming or climate change is beyond absurd and is certainly not scientific. Using that claim to justify destroying our freedom and prosperity is to perpetrate a harmful and destructive hoax.

Powering the Socialist Agenda

Democratic former Vice President Al Gore, a leading perpetrator of the global warming hoax, has enriched himself while flying around the world in fuel-guzzling private jets and riding in parades of limousines to attend global warming conferences, where he preaches against the fuel-guzzling private jets and limousines that transport him.

He heats and cools his own mansion while preaching against the pollution and waste ordinary Americans cause by heating our homes, driving our cars, and flying on commercial jets.

Since the 1970s, socialists have compared global warming to the threat of nuclear war. They predicted that it would cause hundreds of millions of US citizens to starve to death by 1990, and predicted the extinction of 75 percent of all animal species by 1995. Then they predicted it would cause civilization to end by 2000. If our civilization ends soon, the cause will more likely be from socialist governments than from global warming.

Economics professor Walter E. Williams has written that the 2010 world climate summit in Cancun wasn't so much about environmental protection as it was an economic summit at which distribution of the world's resources were negotiated. [xlviii]

The Sun vs. Fiddling With Data

According to a 2015 UPI article by Doug G. Ware, "Solar scientists, armed with the best data yet regarding the activities of the sun, say the Earth is headed for a 'mini ice age' in just 15 years -- something that hasn't happened for three centuries."[xlix]

"Researchers, saying they understand solar cycles better than ever, predict that the sun's normal activity will decrease by 60 percent around 2030 -- triggering the 'mini ice age' that could last for a decade. The last time the Earth was hit by such a lull in solar activity happened 300 years ago, during the Maunder Minimum, which lasted from 1645 to 1715."

"The fiddling with temperature data is the biggest science scandal ever," according to research in an article by Christopher Booker, which continues,

"When future generations look back on the global-warming scare of the past 30 years, nothing will shock them more than the extent to which the official temperature records – on which the entire panic ultimately rested – were systematically "adjusted" to show the Earth as having warmed much more than the actual data justified… This really does begin to look like one of the greatest scientific scandals of all time."[1]

Based on this hoax, Democrats have created rules through the US Environmental Protection Agency (EPA) that increase energy and manufacturing costs, put companies out of business, and kill jobs, including those of coal miners and factory workers.

They block oil drilling and pipeline construction, and force the world's cleanest coal-fired power plants to shut down. Our freedom and prosperity don't matter to them.

It took a surprisingly reasonable 2015 Supreme Court decision in *Michigan v. EPA* to strike down an EPA regulation with no significant environmental impact that would have cost power companies $9.6 billion annually to save just $6 million.

The Democratic Crusade for the Environment

The Democratic "crusade for the environment" is really nothing more than a crusade against freedom and capitalism. Everyone wants clean air and water, so Democrats use MMP to accuse Republicans of wanting to destroy our environment.

Movie and TV stars, channeling the socialists who feed their egos by praising them as if they were actually the heroes they portray, use their acting skills to deliver impassioned speeches about how this hoax is the greatest threat to our species. But the socialists who feed off their celebrity and perpetrate this hoax are the real threat to our freedom and our survival.

Karl Marx wrote that the path to gaining complete communist control requires killing capitalism, and his faithful followers have seized upon this environmental hoax as one of their main weapons to kill capitalism.

29

Limited Temporary Sanity

A Few Steps toward Recovery

Republican George W. Bush, often called Bush 43, defeated
Vice President Al Gore in 2000 to become 43rd US president,
with a split Senate and a Republican majority in the House.
Gore promptly refocused his career on promoting global
warming paranoia.

Bush began rebuilding US military strength, cut taxes, and
proposed partial privatization to reduce continuous misspending
of Social Security taxes. But he also expanded Medicare, and
promoted federally backed mortgage loans.

Bush and Congress enacted the No Child Left Behind Act
(NCLB) in an effort to improve education and provide options
for poor students trapped in low-performing public schools.

Although such control over education is not a federal
responsibility, it was believed that NCLB improved math and
reading achievement among black and Hispanic students.

Attack on America and War on Terrorism

Emboldened by eight years of weak and negligent US
national defense under Clinton, Muslim terrorist group al Qaeda,
led by Saudi millionaire Osama bin Laden, attacked New York
City and Washington DC on September 11, 2001, taking 3,000
lives and destroying billions of dollars in property.

Bush and Congress created the Transportation Security
Administration (TSA), and the Homeland Security Department,
which added bureaucracy for issues that could have been more
efficiently and cost-effectively handled by existing agencies.

In October, Bush launched a War on Terrorism, sending
American troops to hunt down the terrorists and defeat the
repressive Taliban rulers of Afghanistan who had hosted their

training camps. The Taliban was removed from power quickly, while bin Laden and al Qaeda went into hiding.

Iraqi dictator Saddam Hussein, who intimidated political opponents through murder, torture, systematic raping of their wives and mothers, and forcing them to watch their children tortured, cheered al Qaeda. Emboldened by 9/11, he called on all Arabs and all Muslims to attack the US, offered to help any who would, and offered training facilities for terrorists in Iraq.

Saddam Hussein had been using chemical weapons of mass destruction for years, even against Iraqis. Intelligence services believed he had nuclear weapons or soon could, as he continued to block weapons inspections required by the Gulf War treaty.

Congress authorized Bush to use force in Iraq by a 69 percent majority in the House and a 77 percent majority in the Senate on October 16, 2002, with 98 percent of Republican Senators and 58 percent of Democratic Senators, including John Kerry and Hillary Clinton, voting in favor of the resolution.

Even with authorization to act, Bush delayed using force and continued to try other steps. But France, Germany, and Russia, possibly violating the existing UN sanctions, blocked new ones.

Saddam Hussein played negotiating games over inspections, alternately agreeing to them and then kicking weapons inspectors out. Convoy after convoy of trucks suspected to be loaded with weapons, money, and weapons production materials exited Iraq into Syria while Bush made more attempts to negotiate.

Justification for War in Iraq

On March 17, 2003, Bush spoke to his fellow Americans on national TV, gave Saddam Hussein 48 hours to leave Iraq, and explained the justification for military action if he failed to leave.

Iraq had agreed to destroy its weapons of mass destruction and allow continuing weapons inspections as conditions for ending the war in 1991, but through 12 years of diplomacy and a dozen UN resolutions, Iraq had repeatedly failed to comply.

Bush did not claim that Iraq had nuclear weapons, but said the danger was clear: "using chemical, biological or, one day, nuclear weapons, obtained with the help of Iraq, terrorists could fulfill their stated ambitions and kill thousands or hundreds of thousands of innocent people in our country, or any other." [li]

On March 19, 2003, Bush announced to fellow citizens that a coalition led by American forces, with support from over 35 countries, was taking military action "to disarm Iraq, to free its people, and defend the world from a grave danger."

Bush continued, "We will meet that threat now, with our Army, Air Force, Navy, Coast Guard and Marines, so that we do not have to meet it later with armies of fire fighters and police and doctors on the streets of our cities." [lii]

War in Iraq

On the morning of March 20, 2003, every able-brained man and woman in the US who wanted to know, understood that our troops were in Iraq to force compliance with our treaty and end Saddam Hussein's reign of terror. Almost no one wanted war, but a large majority approved of the US action.

Most Americans united behind Bush on the war. US and coalition forces overwhelmed Iraqi forces. Saddam Hussein was captured in December 2003. He was executed by the elected government of Iraq after a military trial in December 2006. But despite initial success, the war was far from over.

Iraqi militias had hidden weapons in many locations before fighting began. Violence broke out between the formerly ruling Sunni Muslims and Shiite Muslims, and more Shiites poured in from Iran. A long insurgency began against US coalition forces.

Another effort to defeat US forces developed at home, when Democrats realized they couldn't win the election of 2004 while most Americans supported Bush on the war. Like the earlier Democrats who attacked Lincoln, trying to win the 1864 election during the Civil War, they were willing to divide our country and surrender in the war for a better chance to win an election.

John Kerry, who had attacked US troops with insults and false allegations during Vietnam, did the same over Iraq, while attacking Bush's motives and actions. Kerry voted against it before he voted for it, but he was against the war. After he lost the election, Democrats were heavily invested in US defeat.

Iraq held its first free election in fifty years in January 2005, but MMP buried most positive news about war developments and about weapons US troops found, promoted lies about Bush's justifications and motives, and painted US victories as defeats.

Before Congress approved the successful 2007 troop surge, Kerry and Hillary Clinton vehemently opposed winning the war, and repeatedly proposed withdrawal (surrender). Hillary and others shrieked insults at our military leaders, and attacked our commanding general with false accusations.

After the unquestionable success of the troop surge, Bush began gradually drawing down the number of US troops in Iraq, with the situation there stable in late 2007.

Establishing freedom and democratic elections in Iraq and Afghanistan cost many US lives and dollars, but made the world more stable and safer for Americans, until all the gains were reversed by Barack Obama, Hillary Clinton, and John Kerry.

US soldiers who gave their lives for our country protected us. We can never know how many American lives they saved, but there would almost certainly have been more terrorist attacks on US cities if the Clinton policy of no military action except to divert attention from his personal misconduct had continued.

Bush and members of his administration made mistakes, as leaders do in every war, and there was misconduct by a small number of US troops, which was quickly stopped.

But no Bush mistake compares with what happened when enemies of freedom and the US military took control after the 2008 election and surrendered almost everything our troops had won, to focus their efforts on controlling US citizens.

Bush's actions in defeating Saddam Hussein and driving Osama bin Laden into hiding shifted the battleground from US cities to Afghanistan and Iraq, and prevented further devastating attacks on US soil.

Mortgage Loan Crisis, Recession, and Stimulus

The 2008 mortgage loan crisis and recession arose from many factors: excessive federal taxation and spending, federal collusion with banks, housing bills enacted under Carter and Bush 41 which pushed banks into high-risk loans, and Bush 43's promotion of them.

Unfortunately, Bush and Congress, with both the Senate and House under Democratic control, reacted with $168 billion in "stimulus" spending, federal takeover of two government lending arms, and a $700 billion taxpayer bail-out of private lenders.

Safer and Stronger Despite Problems

Bush restored the US to the role of responsible world leader and defender of freedom after another Democratic president's dismantling of US national defense.

Bush's war plan was too ambitious and costly, and he made mistakes. A more limited focus like those used by Reagan and Bush 41 might have better served US interests. But his actions made the US stronger and the world safer for Americans through the first few years of the subsequent dismantling of those gains.

Bush 43 allowed the federal government's size and spending to grow too much, but reduced its overreach in some areas, even while compromising with Democrats in Congress to be able to carry out basic national defense responsibilities.

Despite bad economic developments at the end of his term, our country was better able to defend freedom when Bush left, and in better shape overall than most Americans understood. The US economy was salvageable until Democrats took control.

Next: Destruction of Our Freedom

What has happened since Bush left office is a national disaster that is extinguishing the security, individual freedom and natural rights of all Americans.

30

Final Destruction of Freedom in Progress

Destruction of Remaining Freedom and Rights

Democrat Barack Hussein Obama promised he would "fundamentally transform" our country. Taking office as 44th US President in 2009, he set out to complete the transformation from freedom to socialism that FDR and LBJ had led, and for which the Clintons, Kerry, and other Democrats had worked.

They had destroyed most of the limits on federal power before Obama assumed leadership to finish the transformation. Like Marx, Stalin, and Mao, they regard our property and money as rightfully belonging to the central government. They promise to take it from "the rich" and redistribute it, but they take it from every rich and poor person with an income, except themselves.

Obama appointed a cabinet of Democrats and created a shadow cabinet of communist and socialist "czars," who couldn't win confirmation to cabinet posts even from Senate Democrats. He once joked that his job would be easier if he were president of China. Unfortunately, he wasn't really joking.

House Speaker Nancy Pelosi and Senate Majority Leader Harry Reid rallied their Democratic majorities in Congress to help him attack the remaining limits on federal power.

Payoffs to Political Contributors

Using billions of tax dollars, Obama seized control of General Motors (GM). He fired management and subordinated the rights of bond holders to those of labor unions, effectively stealing GM assets from many Americans to pay off union bosses who fund Democratic campaigns with union dues--the same union bosses who helped create the financial problems both GM and Chrysler were facing.

Without his wrongful intervention, GM assets would have been bought out of bankruptcy and most jobs could have been

128

saved. But Democrats feared losing millions of dollars in campaign funds that union bosses extort from the workers.

Cash for Clunkers cost billions more tax dollars, destroyed hundreds of thousands of serviceable cars, and hurt consumers by raising prices of used cars, in another payoff to union bosses.

His union Card Check rule and some of his appointments were such extreme attacks on the rights on non-union workers that even the Senate controlled by Democrats blocked them.

Billions more for Obama's "stimulus" plan stimulated only US national debt and the wealth of his political supporters. His meddling in Chrysler's bankruptcy helped put many independent car dealerships out of business, and their employees out of jobs.

Federal Collusion with Banks

Obama and Congress enacted a credit card law that invades the privacy of citizens and gives more control to bureaucrats and banks that were already "too big to fail." The most repressive banking bill since the Great Depression authorized thousands of new regulations, added red tape, and made federal takeover of companies easier. Economic recovery is not their priority.

Government Ownership of Citizens through Health Care

"Obamacare," the 2010 socialist Democratic law to control American citizens through our health care, is one of the most destructive expansions of federal power in US history.

Senate Democrats raced to pass it before a Republican could be elected to replace an appointed Democrat and stop them from forcing it on US citizens. All Senate Democrats voted for it, and all Republicans voted against it. Citizen protests persuaded 34 House Democrats to join all 178 Republicans who voted against it, but it still passed in the House 219-212.

This disaster for health care, like "Hillary care" that they failed to impose, attacks our most basic freedom, ownership of ourselves. No one has legally exercised so much control over others here since slavery was abolished.

Obamacare was enacted by Democrats, the party of slavery, over opposition by Republicans, the party that abolished slavery.

129

It has enriched hospitals and insurance companies beyond belief, and made them our masters, in partnership with government.

This clearly unconstitutional law has been upheld twice by the Supreme Court, in defiance of the Constitution that created the Court's authority. Emboldened by these rulings, Democrats have stepped up their attacks on free enterprise and religious freedom, including against the Little Sisters of the Poor.

Anti-Military Radicals in Control of National Defense

During his campaign, Obama supported Hillary, John Kerry, and other Democrats as they claimed that victory in Iraq was impossible, urged surrender, and verbally attacked our troops.

Obama made it clear he had no serious intention of doing his first job of leading US national defense. By appointing Hillary Clinton to succeed Condoleezza Rice as Secretary of State, he replaced a first rate defender of freedom with an untrustworthy politician, focused on extinguishing our freedom at home.

The Benghazi debacle is just one example of her negligence, incompetence, and disdain for US troops. She surrendered a US embassy, got an ambassador and three US troops killed, lied about it, and then promoted a completely fabricated political story about a video to cover her misdeeds.

Surrendering after Victory

Under Bush, US troops won wars in Iraq and Afghanistan. Three years later, Obama withdrew all our troops from Iraq, surrendering almost everything they won in both wars. He and Hillary disrespected the soldiers who died for our country, and abandoned many billions of dollars in US military equipment which is now in the hands of our enemies. The chaos and terrorism that have ensued threaten our security today.

Obama appointed John Kerry to continue Hillary's trashing of US national security. Both have helped Obama make the world more dangerous for Americans.

Democrats are reducing US Army strength, even as threats against us grow and our enemies attack US recruiting offices and military installations within our own borders.

Obama's bizarre courting of Cuba's communist rulers hurts US national security, and emboldens the Castro brothers to take more violent actions against human rights activists within Cuba.

Appeasement of Iran and War within US Borders

Obama and Kerry have followed the path of British Prime Minister Neville Chamberlain, who appeased Hitler before World War II, hoping to prevent war with the Nazis.

As Republicans made bumbling attempts to stop them, they committed us to appeasement that will help Iran's Islamic terrorist regime in their efforts to destroy Israel, threaten other US allies in the region, and launch nuclear attacks against our own cities. Kerry bragged that no one could stop them.

Obama claims he's not a Muslim, but his father and step-father were, and he attended a Muslim school. His actions will help radical Muslims achieve their dreams of killing Jews and Americans, so whether he's a Muslim or not doesn't matter.

While he and Kerry appease them, Iranian Muslims post videos about destroying us and chant "Death to America!"

Their actions also support the Muslim war against us through "resettlement jihad," settling here and then demanding to be governed by Islamic "sharia law" instead of by US laws.

Brigitte Gabriel of Act for America wrote, "Since day one, the Obama Administration has engaged with those who seek not to 'reach an accommodation with the West but to destroy it.' This has resulted in a global image of U.S. weakness and vulnerability. American citizens must take action to reverse course. We must elect a competent, strong and respected President who understands the jihadist threat both at home and abroad, and who is not afraid (or unwilling) to confront it." [liii]

Refusal to Enforce Immigration Laws

Obama enables the invasion of illegal aliens from across our Mexican border. Many are violent criminals, but Democrats oppose securing our border and enforcing US immigration laws to increase the number of people on welfare and to benefit from the potential for fraudulent votes of illegal aliens.

Elite Democrats who live in secure communities protected from the murders, rapes, and drug violence that result, don't care about the ordinary citizens they expose to crime any more than Democratic plantation owners cared about Americans who opposed slavery. The Obamas, Clintons, and Kerrys don't need to worry much about violent crimes on their streets.

Before Obama, no President openly refused to enforce US immigration laws he had sworn to uphold. But the House won't impeach him because Senate Democrats can block his removal.

MMP Insults Immigrants and Black Americans

Immigrants who come here legally, learn our language, respect our laws, assimilate into our culture, and achieve US citizenship are legitimate American citizens. But Democratic MMP insults and demeans legal and law-abiding immigrants by constantly referring to illegal aliens as "immigrants."

They insult and demean black Americans by comparing their long quest for equal rights to the Democratic quest to gain votes by creating special rights for illegal aliens and others.

Abuses of Power

Abuses of power by Obama continue daily. One blatant example is his administration's use of the Internal Revenue Service (IRS) to harass private citizens that Obama sees as politically dangerous to Democrats, such as tea party members.

Two other cases, each more serious than Nixon's Watergate actions, involve "lost" e-mails, apparently destroyed to cover up evidence of IRS misconduct, and evidence of Hillary Clinton's misconduct as Secretary of State related to the Benghazi scandal. Under Obama, abuses of power are just "business as usual."

Unlimited National Debt

Limited tax is necessary, and some debt is reasonable. But by ignoring Constitutional limits, Obama and Democrats have made our taxes and debt unreasonable, unfair, and dangerous.

Unlimited national debt can make it impossible to defend our freedom. We can't even stop its growth without a dramatic change. Democrats want us to pay even more or stop spending on national defense, but many Americans still want freedom.

US national debt is $19 trillion, or $60,000 for each man, woman, and child of our 320 million population. The financial collapse in Greece, by comparison, involves $350 billion in debt, or $32,000 for each person of their 11 million population.

Obama, Democrats, and compromising Republicans are stealing the money to get by from our children and grandchildren by borrowing it, so we can leave the debt for them to pay, imposing taxation without representation against children who can't even vote to defend themselves.

If our government becomes unable to defend us from foreign aggression, maintain civil order, and protect basic human rights, our children and grandchildren won't inherit anything but our debt and a cruel punishment for our failure to maintain freedom.

Promoting Racism, Harming Black Americans

The transformation from freedom to socialism harms all of us, regardless of color, but Obama's policies particularly harm black people. His presidency has been a disaster for America, but worse for black Americans, although few blame him.

Obama has expanded LBJ's War on Freedom, adding to the millions of black Americans trapped on the modern Democratic plantation of welfare, food stamps, and public housing, and kept black children trapped in dysfunctional public schools.

Instead of working to lift black Americans, Obama and his advisor Al Sharpton, former civil rights leader Jesse Jackson, and others encourage racism, racial violence, rioting, and confrontations with police to keep many blacks segregated from white Americans and under the control of Democrats.

It is sadly ironic that the first black US president and his supporters have spent his entire presidency promoting race riots and hatred between black and white Americans.

Gun Control

The purpose of gun control is to keep citizens from being able to defend themselves. During segregation, it kept black men from shooting back at the easy targets Democrats presented in the white sheets and hoods they wore as KKK terrorists.

Gun control is necessary to keep the people of North Korea, China, and Russia under control of their communist oppressors. Obama and other Democrats want to use it here for the same purpose, so they tell us that gun control is for our own good and the only way to stop the violence their policies have created.

However, James Craig, the black Police Chief of Detroit, who returned to his hometown to clean up the mess government created there and restore public safety, encourages responsible, legal ownership of guns by citizens to help accomplish that. [liv]

We would all like to see a day when citizens don't need guns to defend ourselves against criminals, but the more important reason we need them, as our founders often pointed out, is to prevent having to defend ourselves against our government.

Fundamentally Transforming (Breaking) the Constitution

Obama's appointments of two extreme socialists as Supreme Court Justices are his most permanently destructive actions. They were not appointed to fulfill the responsibilities of Justices and live up to their oaths of office, but to defy their oaths of office and help transform us from freedom to socialism.

Sonia Sotomayor and Elena Kagan have been given the power to hurt all Americans for as long as they live by further destroying the US Constitution's ability to protect our freedom. Senate Democrats are the ones who confirmed them, but a few Senate Republicans are at least partly to blame for stopping other Republicans from blocking their confirmations.

Obama has nominated another destroyer freedom to fill the Supreme Court vacancy left by the recent death of Justice Antonin Scalia, who was one of only three justices living up to their oaths of office by upholding the US Constitution. But the Senate must do its duty to defend the Constitution by blocking this attempt to permanently destroy our freedom, and should stop Obama from making any more judicial appointments.

31

Supreme Court's Destruction of the Constitution that Created It

Basis of the Supreme Court's Authority

The entire United States government, led by Congress, the president, and the Supreme Court, exists only by authority of the US Constitution. Through the Constitution, the people of the United States granted our government leaders all of the powers they legitimately possess.

The people and the States created our federal government to secure and defend their freedom and enable them to pass the benefits of freedom along to their descendants.

All people possess natural rights granted by our Creator. States derive many powers from the consent of their citizens, but the federal government has only limited powers, granted by the people and the States through the US Constitution.

The US government doesn't legitimately possess any powers not granted by the Constitution. The first ten amendments were written to further ensure that it would not interfere with the rights of the people or States by assuming powers not granted.

To ensure that the limits remain in place to protect citizens, the Constitution requires that all legislators, and all executive and judicial Officers of the US and of all the States "shall be bound by Oath or Affirmation, to support this Constitution."

Each Supreme Court justice has sworn or affirmed that he or she will "bear full faith and allegiance" to the US Constitution. But the justices regularly violate their oaths of office by assuming powers not granted to them.

Court Unconstitutionally Limits Individual Freedom

Supreme Court justices began to unconstitutionally limit the rights of Americans before the Civil War. In the Dred Scott case of 1857, Democratic Justices ruled that a black man could never be a US citizen, regardless of whether he was a slave or free, partly because a citizen has a right to own and carry a gun.

The Court limited the rights of all citizens in the late 1800s to deny the rights of black citizens under the 14th Amendment. Contrived justifications to uphold Jim Crow laws kept black men unarmed, as Democrats suppressed their Republican votes.

Justices ignored the purpose of the first ten amendments and began "interpreting" them as if they had been written to create, define, and limit the rights of the people.

Court Wrongfully Expands Limits on Federal Power

Enumerated powers were granted to government to provide for the common defense and general welfare of the United States. "General welfare" meant actions for the welfare of all citizens, not just for just one group of citizens or one State.

Despite rulings that wrongfully limited the rights of States and citizens, most limits on the powers granted to the federal government were understood and generally respected for 148 years from 1788 until 1936.

"Congress has not unlimited powers to provide for the general welfare, but only those specifically enumerated." -- Thomas Jefferson, 1817 [lv]

But in their 1936 *US v Butler* decision, the Court made the incredible new "discovery" that the words "general welfare" conferred a power separate and distinct from those enumerated, empowering Congress to enact laws and spend for any public purpose for the general welfare of the country. Their absurd ruling was that the enumerated powers didn't limit anything.

Of course, if this were true, there wouldn't have been any reason to enumerate the powers. The framers could have just written that Congress can do anything they want for the general welfare of the country. If the Constitution had been written to agree with the Butler decision, it would have never been ratified.

This decision and their 1937 ruling under the duress of FDR's intimidation in *Helvering v. Davis* have given politicians false justification for transforming the United Sates from a land of freedom to a land of unlimited government control.

Since the *Butler* decision, the Supreme Court has ignored the Constitution, the Declaration of Independence, and the other writings of our founders who created them.

Presidents and Congress ignore the Constitution to whatever extent they find convenient, and to whatever extent the Supreme Court fails to uphold its limits.

Supreme Court justices have repeatedly ruled against the Constitution that created their authority, perverting the purpose of our government. Instead of protecting our freedom, they have transformed it into the main force destroying our freedom.

Supreme Court Places Itself Above the Constitution

The US Supreme Court was not granted authority to change the US Constitution the way English courts have changed their unwritten constitution for centuries under the tradition of English Common Law. Our founders freed themselves from England, and established a written Constitution to protect our freedom.

The Supreme Court's only legitimate authority is to apply the law correctly; to rule only within the limits of the Constitution that created it, and not to change the Constitution.

No provision of the Constitution gives previous rulings of the Supreme Court, called precedents, a higher position of authority than the Constitution itself.

By ignoring the Constitution and ruling according to their precedents, the Court illogically places its own authority above the Constitution, ruling against the law that created the Court. Without the authority granted by the Constitution, the Court's rulings are based upon no authority whatsoever.

The primary author of our Declaration of Independence warned against the Court's tyranny almost 200 years ago. In 1821, Thomas Jefferson wrote,

"The germ of dissolution of our federal government is in the constitution of the federal judiciary; an irresponsible body, (for impeachment is scarcely a scare-crow) working like gravity by

137

night and by day, gaining a little today and a little tomorrow, and advancing its noiseless step like a thief, over the field of jurisdiction, until all shall be usurped from the States, and the government of all be consolidated into one." [lvi]

Jefferson was correct. The Supreme Court has worked like gravity to bring down the Constitution's ability to protect the natural rights of the people. Like a thief in the night, it is silent except at dramatic moments when it strikes devastating blows to our rights. Threat of impeachment has not caused Supreme Court Justices to rule within the Constitution, but it should.

The Constitution states that justices "shall hold their Offices during good Behaviour," but violating one's oath of office is not "good behaviour." Justices who take office only to defy their oaths, destroy the Constitution's ability to protect freedom, and impose their own will, should be impeached and removed.

If Jefferson were alive today, he would almost certainly demand that justices who rule in violation of the Constitution be impeached and removed from office.

Justices, Injustices, and Rogues

During recent years, only three of the nine US Supreme Court justices have consistently demonstrated respect for the US Constitution and made rulings within the authority granted them. They were Antonin Scalia, appointed by Reagan, Clarence Thomas, appointed by Bush 41, and Samuel Alito, appointed by Bush 43. Unfortunately for the freedom of all Americans, Justice Antonin Scalia passed away on February 13, 2016.

Four were appointed by Democratic Presidents only to destroy our freedom and natural rights. The socialist "injustices" who consistently violate their oaths of office are Ruth Bader Ginsberg and Stephen Breyer, appointed by Clinton, and Sonya Sotomayor and Elena Kagan, appointed by Obama.

Two rogue justices apparently believe their own authority supersedes the Constitution, and that their job is to make US laws conform to their personal beliefs. Their appointments were the mistakes of Republican Presidents. Anthony Kennedy was Reagan's third choice after Senate Democrats defeated his first two choices because they respected the Constitution, and Chief Justice John Roberts was Bush 43's mistake.

Three recent decisions demonstrate how the rogue justices use the consistent anti-Constitutional votes of the Court's Democrats to destroy specific freedoms as they choose.

Two Unconstitutional "Obamacare" Decisions

There is clearly no Constitutional authority for the 2010 law known as Obamacare, which effectively grants the government ownership interest in our bodies and penalizes citizens for not buying government-approved health insurance at inflated prices.

In their 2012 decision, the Court's four socialists effectively held that Congress and the President have unlimited power. The three justices who respected the Constitution dissented, joined by rogue Kennedy. But instead of ruling within the limits of his power, rogue Chief Justice Roberts joined the four socialists, and then effectively re-wrote the law to make it enforceable.

The 2015 decision again upheld unlimited federal power over citizens, effectively ruling that the president can change the meaning of words in laws if they aren't convenient to him. In his absurd ruling, Roberts re-wrote a second section of the law.

Amending a Constitutional Amendment

In a 2015 decision, rogue Justice Kennedy used the votes of the four socialists to usurp the power of States and strike blows against freedom of speech and religion. His ruling defied logic, Constitutional limits, and the First and Tenth Amendments.

Kennedy ruled that the 14th Amendment, written to grant citizenship and equal protection to former slaves, also granted Kennedy a special power to re-define words. Kennedy decreed that all 50 States must apply his new definition of "marriage" to relationships between two men or two women. Even Roberts, the re-writer, was baffled.

Gays and lesbians, as they wish to be called, are people with natural rights, too, but theirs don't supersede the rights of others.

No one was denying such individuals the ability to vote, sit at a lunch counter, eat in a restaurant, or rent a room. Those who

139

pretend this is such an issue insult and demean black Americans and others who have had to fight for equal protection. This distortion of reality by the Supreme Court imposes the will of a small minority on others, and denies equal protection of rights.

This decree, on authority created in Kennedy's imagination, provides ammunition to socialist Democrats in their war against the rights of other citizens, and they're using it forcefully.

The Supreme Court decree that made abortion available on demand at taxpayer expense and this one requiring all States to redefine marriage are based on no authority whatsoever.

The Struggle for One Reasonable Decision

A 2015 decision in which the Supreme Court followed the Constitution demonstrates how close we are to losing all our freedom while four members of the Court remain committed to destroying the Constitution's ability to protect our rights.

An EPA administrative law that would have no measurable impact on the environment decreed that power companies spend $9.6 billion per year to save $6 million in energy costs. The four socialists stood behind the EPA, requiring both rogue justices to rule by law to protect citizens from this excessive penalty for socialist climate change paranoia.

How The Supreme Court Has Replaced Slavery

Since the 13th, 14th, and 15th Amendments repaired the flaw of slavery, the Supreme Court has replaced slavery as the most harmful flaw in the US Constitution.

In his 1848 book, *The Law*, Frederic Bastiat's description of what French socialists were doing to natural rights fits what our Supreme Court and our elected leaders have done to the US Constitution, the law designed to protect our freedom and rights.

"The law, I say, not only turned from its proper purpose but made to follow an entirely contrary purpose! The law become the weapon of every kind of greed! Instead of checking crime, the law itself guilty of the evils it is supposed to punish!" [lvii]

32

Mass Media Propaganda and Censorship

Our Sources of Information

A multi-billion dollar industry exists to bring us news and entertainment through TV, radio, newspaper, and the internet, collectively called mass media.

They sell us on becoming their audience by providing the news, sports, and entertainment we want. We provide the ratings and circulation they need to sell their advertising at a profit, so their advertisers can sell us their products and services.

They use words like fast, accurate, complete, unbiased, and factual to sell us on using them as our news sources, and we stay connected to be entertained and to know what's happening.

The news we get affects our perception and understanding of events. We expect it to be complete, accurate, and unbiased, because that's how it's sold to us, and our freedom of the press leads us believe that's how it should be.

Freedom of the Press Has Bitten the Dust

Unfortunately, our freedom of the press was buried long ago with most of our other rights. Our federal government doesn't officially censor our news or replace it with propaganda, but Democrats do that unofficially through Mass Media Propaganda (MMP) in partnership with the huge socialist government bureaucracy they've built to control us.

In China, Russia, Cuba, Iran, North Korea, and many other countries, freedom of the press isn't an issue. It simply doesn't exist. During the 1960s, Americans ridiculed the communist propaganda, so unbelievable that it sounded silly, from countries where all the "news" was controlled by their government.

At the same time, socialist Democrats were transforming our free press into the MMP machine they use to control us today.

Many journalists were drawn to news and big government in the 1960s with good intentions. They wanted to stop the war, segregation, and racial discrimination. They believed many of LBJ's lies, and failed to see the damage he was doing.

Now they run the companies that bring us the "news." They still believe the same lies fifty years later and refuse to see the truth, partly because they have a financial interest in keeping the damage growing. Our free press is nothing more than a charade.

Mass Media has a financial interest in supporting Democrats who bring us big government. The bigger our government, the more of our money flows into Mass Media through it. And they profit from political spending on many issues over which the federal government does not exercise legitimate authority.

Mass Media treats Republicans as enemies partly because respect for Constitutional limits would shrink government and decrease the cash flow to Mass Media.

News and Commercials

Marketing and advertising professionals use repetition and frequency in Mass Media to make us believe their messages. The more often we hear their messages, the more likely we are to believe them, whether true or false. Repetition and frequency can make people believe almost anything.

Mass Media Propaganda uses them to make us believe almost anything, too. They build scoundrels into heroes and tear down heroes to make us think they're scoundrels.

They often brag about how many people they've fooled with follow-up stories about their contrived surveys. Their bragging often begins with, "Most Americans now believe that..."

Crossover between propaganda and entertainment occurs naturally, since TV "journalists" are mostly just actors skilled at reading from electronic prompters while pretending to care.

The focus of broadcast news is on propaganda and telling us how to live our lives. The game shows, comedies, reality shows, and sports we see between propaganda blasts numb many minds to the fact that our freedom is almost gone.

No Bias in Mass Media

Some complain about bias in the news, but it doesn't exist. Bias describes a leaning toward one side of an issue, and implies inclusion of more than one point of view. With the exception of one network, there is only one point of view in mass media.

Treatment of Candidates

Republicans are confronted with insults and accusations, while Democrats are greeted as heroes by their adoring fans.

If a Republican candidate makes a comment that sounds uninformed, it's a national crisis, but it's not for a Democrat.

Republican 2008 vice presidential candidate Sarah Palin was slapped with confrontational questions at every turn. Even slight mistakes in her answers were played repeatedly for days.

They didn't ask Democratic presidential candidate Barack Obama many questions, but when he volunteered that he was campaigning in "all 57 states," they quickly changed the subject and buried the story. If Palin had said something nearly as ignorant, we'd still be hearing it with every mention of her name.

2016 election propaganda is already bad, but just beginning.

The Garbage They Feed Us

The late Frank Zappa's song, "I am the Slime," is about the vile and pernicious slime oozing from our TVs to control us. But the slime oozing from our TVs today is worse.

MMP uses the playground technique of name-calling against anyone whose honesty offends them.

Anyone who promotes global warming hysteria is a "scientist." Anyone who doesn't is a "global warming denier."

Anyone who wants to stop Muslim terrorist attacks on Americans is called an "Islamaphobe."

Anyone who opposes special gay rights is a "homophobe."

It would be impossible to clean up all the slime we're fed, and MMP feeds us more every day. But let's tackle just a few examples of garbage they feed us with repetition and frequency:

To promote their campaign against our right to self-defense, any violent criminal act by a person with a gun is called "gun violence," and the violent criminal is called a "gunman."

The murders of five unarmed people at US military recruiting offices by a radical Muslim were called a "rampage" by a gunman, instead of an Islamic terrorist attack.

A person shot to death while pointing a gun at a cop is a deceased violent criminal, but called a "police shooting victim."

Destruction caused by a violent criminal fleeing police is blamed on a "police chase," not on the criminal.

Criminals looting, burning buildings, and murdering people during riots are referred to as "protesters."

Beheadings and other violent murders by Muslim terrorists and other criminals are called "executions."

Despite their fabrications, the deadly Obama / Hillary Benghazi disaster was not caused by US free speech in a video.

The "science" is not settled. God and nature control the earth's climate, not Democrats and the US EPA.

The people illegally flooding across our border from Mexico are not "undocumented immigrants," but illegal aliens.

Equality under the law is not the same as trying to force socialist-engineered equal outcome.

Federal spending and federal control are not the only two solutions to every real or imagined problem.

Income inequality is not necessarily unfair. Most NBA stars should earn more than a high school basketball coach.

If you don't like being a man or a woman, you can attempt or pretend to change, but no one else should be expected or obliged to cheer your personal battle against God and nature.

A teenage boy was not "brave" to commit suicide because his parents refused to pretend he was a girl.

A person who opposes Planned Parenthood for aborting live children and selling baby parts is not waging a "war on women."

"Diversity" is a word socialists use to keep us segregated and justify racially discriminatory policies.

Tea Party members who advocate limited government, fiscal responsibility, and free markets are not "racists" or "terrorists."

Black men who advocate freedom, respect for the US Constitution, and responsible government are not "Uncle Toms."

But Barack Obama, Al Sharpton, Jesse Jackson, and others who cheer government ownership of black Americans may be.

Academia: Worse than MMP

Colleges and universities we support with tax dollars have become cesspools of censorship and socialism, censoring speech that promotes the protection of freedom.

Their focus is socialist indoctrination, as professors preach against capitalists who pay for their high salaries and benefits.

MMP, low quality education, and socialist indoctrination at a public university recently came together in a newspaper column.

A graduate student wrote that forcing all of us to pay Planned Parenthood for her birth control of choice so she can enjoy sex with her boyfriend more freely does not affect us in any way, and we should butt out. She wrote that Republican objections are just part of a war on women. [lviii]

Banning Confederate Symbols of Democrat History

MMP recently blamed a racist murder by a white whacko on Confederate symbols, and implied that all whites are racists.

MMP promotes destroying all traces of the Confederacy, much as the Taliban destroys symbols of history they don't like in Afghanistan. Democrats want to take down Confederate flags, tear down monuments to Confederate leaders, and even dig up and remove their dead bodies from their graves.

Why? Because the Confederates were all Democrats. They want to erase history and evidence of who Democrats really are.

A better solution would be to erase all Democrats from public office.

33

Why Black Lives Don't Matter to One Party

Black Lives Mattered to Democrats Only as Slaves

When the modern Democratic Party was founded in the 1820s by Andrew Jackson and other slave owners to protect slavery, the only thing about black people that mattered to Democratic leaders was their value as slaves.

A core value of the Democratic Party, and their justification for slavery, was that the black race was inferior to the white race, and black people were unfit for anything but slavery. Black lives didn't matter to Democrats.

Slavery to Segregation, Democrats Just Shifted Gears

After Republicans abolished slavery, freed the slaves, and established their citizenship, black people were Republicans.

When Democrats regained power, all that mattered to them about black people was subjugating them under segregation, and suppressing their votes to keep Republicans out of power.

A New Democratic Plan to Control Black Americans

When free black Americans and other Republicans were finally on the brink of defeating segregation, Democrats fought back hard, causing the racial violence of the 1960s.

LBJ had no intention of giving black Americans a fair chance through equal protection, but he had a plan to turn black power into Democrat voting power.

He led Democrats to finally help Republicans pass civil rights and voting rights laws, but he subverted those laws by "helping" black people through oppressive federal programs.

Replacing the KKK with MMP

Democrats didn't love black people any more in 1964 than during the previous 100 years of segregation and oppression, but LBJ had a more ambitious plan to keep them segregated, keep them from voting for Republicans, and use their votes to help him gain more control over all Americans.

His formula, borrowed from FDR, was to keep the crisis going, blame it on someone else, use tax dollars to buy votes, and make the people in crisis feel dependent on Democrats.

The crisis of violence against black victims continued, from the crime produced by his welfare state. Many black men were arrested, as they had been under Jim Crow laws.

The difference was that black victims were being killed by other black men instead of by the KKK, and black men were being arrested for committing those crimes.

Democrats used Mass Media Propaganda (MMP) to obscure those details and blame the violence against black people on unspecified white "racists."

Then Democrats began calling Republicans who opposed de facto segregation under their welfare state "racists," and blamed the arrests of black men on police who tried to stop the violence. MMP helped establish those public images.

Propaganda can make people believe almost anything, and with MMP as their new enforcement arm, Democrats didn't need the KKK anymore. Black lives still didn't matter to Democrats.

Black Americans on the Modern Democratic Plantation

Democrats used the Department of Housing and Urban Development (HUD), to control where poor black people could live. The projects quickly became breeding grounds for crime, where criminals were the only people who felt safe.

Welfare, food stamps, and public housing destroyed black families, encouraged crime, built dependence on Democrats, and kept millions of black Americans segregated in urban slums.

Democrats used Planned Parenthood abortions to control the number of black and other "undesirable" babies born.

They have spent trillions of federal dollars fighting a 50 year War on Poverty to make millions of black Americans dependent on them, but the poverty rate of roughly 15 percent remains.

147

Those dollars haven't helped us achieve MLK's dream, but they've helped Democrats gain control over all Americans, and have made Democratic leaders rich and powerful.

Fraudulent Education in Public Schools

Education is one of the best ways to improve a person's life. School boards, school administrations, and teachers' unions in large US cities are dominated by Democrats, including black Democrats. Those districts spend many dollars per student, but have failed to equally educate black students for decades.

From the school boards and teachers all the way up to our president, Democrats hurt black students by expecting less, demanding less, failing to maintain school discipline, passing them through schools with fraudulent diplomas, and opposing school vouchers that would give their parents a choice.

Instead of educating black students to prepare them for success, Democratic politicians, teachers, and former civil rights organizations falsely attack academic performance standards as racially discriminatory and demand lower college admissions standards for black students. When you obviously expect less of someone, he is less likely to achieve.

Economics professor, math tutor, and author Walter E. Williams is a black father who wants black students to excel.

Williams writes that academic tests show the average black twelfth grader performs at the level of the average white seventh-or-eighth grader, and that black students "score at least 100 points lower than whites in each of the assessment areas—critical reading, math, and writing" on SAT tests.[lix]

Williams notes there are factors the schools can't control. For him to do well, "someone must make the student do his homework. Someone must see to it that he gets eight to nine hours of sleep. Someone has to fix him a wholesome breakfast and ensure that he gets to school on time and respects and obeys his teachers." [lx]

But Williams calls it "academic fraud" when schools grant diplomas attesting that students have mastered twelfth grade levels of reading, writing, and arithmetic, when the students can't perform above eighth grade levels. In most cases, neither students nor their parents are aware of this achievement gap.[lxi]

Respecting and obeying teachers is essential to good education. On school discipline, Williams wrote that "most schools identified as 'persistently dangerous' are predominately black schools," and that "nationally, the black four year high school graduation rate is 52 percent." [lxii]

Economist, professor, and author Thomas Sowell, who is also black, wrote that discipline in school helped him achieve success. Sowell objected to the Obama Justice Department's extortion of Minneapolis Public Schools, forcing them to ration discipline by racial quotas, "apparently under the assumption that black males could not possibly commit any more offenses than Asian females or any other set of students."

Sowell wrote that politically, "any time they can depict blacks as victims and depict themselves as their rescuers, that means an opportunity to get out the black votes for Democrats."

"Anyone with common sense knows that letting a kid get away with bad behavior is an open invitation to worse behavior in the future. Punishing a kid for misbehavior in school when he is 10 years old may reduce the chances that he will have to be sent to prison when he is 20 years old.

"Letting kids who are behavior problems in schools grow up to become hoodlums and then criminals is no favor to them or to the black community. Moreover, it takes no more than a small fraction of troublemakers in a class to make it impossible to give that class a decent education. And for many poor people, whether black or white, education is their one big chance to escape poverty."[lxiii]

Williams points out that blacks dominate in sports, where competition is fierce, to the extent that 80 percent of professional basketball players and 65 percent of professional football players are black, and that black players are among the highest paid.

Williams believes that black students would rise to the top with equal competition in school. "I'm betting that a significant number of black youngsters would prosper in such an environment, just as they prosper in the highly competitive sports and entertainment environments." [lxiv]

Sowell wrote that Dunbar High School, a black school in Washington D.C. before school integration, proved that theory. Dunbar scores were regularly higher than scores at two of the three white high schools in the city. For several decades, four-fifths of Dunbar graduates went on to college, and "at one time, Dunbar graduates could get into Dartmouth or Harvard without having to take an entrance exam." [lxv]

Black students who want to succeed have proven they can excel in schools that expect and demand excellence.

One good way for children get a better education is through school vouchers that allow their parents to choose better schools. To benefit from the opportunity, though, parents must ensure that their children conform to the policies of the school they choose, and must help them do their best. Schools accepting vouchers should never change or lower their academic standards to treat voucher students differently.

Democrats oppose letting parents use vouchers to help their children escape failing schools, because union dues from public school teachers provide millions of their campaign dollars.

A recent news article featured a black grandfather who had camped outside a school for two weeks to register his grandson for kindergarten in a good public school. [lxvi] Cincinnati Public Schools don't provide good schools for all students because the socialist Democrats on the school board misspend tax dollars.

Priorities they place above educating children are building new schools instead of bothering to maintain existing ones, and hiring only construction contractors who pay inflated union wages, to pay off union bosses who bankroll Democratic election campaigns with union dues.

President Obama's children attend private schools while he and his administration fight against letting parents of poor black students choose the same opportunity.

Williams asks why 44 percent of public school teachers in Chicago and Philadelphia have their children enrolled in private schools (35 percent in Baltimore, 34 percent in San Francisco).[lxvii]

One of my friends who is black was a highly-regarded math teacher in public schools for twenty years. His daughter attends a private school because the parents of her classmates make them do their homework and demand good behavior, just as he does.

MMP Promotes Racial Distrust and Hatred

To give us the impression that most crimes against black people are committed by white "racists," MMP news stories almost never report the races of perpetrators and victims of violent crimes except when the perpetrator is white and the victim is black.

In the relatively few cases where the victim is black and the perpetrator is white, MMP excitedly reports those details of the crime with repetition and frequency for days or weeks, with bogus accusations of racist motives and wild conjectures about what caused the perpetrator to hate black people.

But the pervasive white on black violent crime of the KKK days mostly ceased when Democrats took off their white sheets and hoods, and replaced their KKK terrorism with MMP.

The Truth About Who Kills Black Americans

Black Americans are 13 percent of the US population, but about 50 percent of murder victims.

Walter E. Williams, who served in Korea, wrote that there were fifteen times as many black murder victims on our streets between 1976 and 2011 than the number of black men killed in Korea, Vietnam, and every war since.[lxviii] A young black man may have a better chance of surviving military service during a war than surviving life on our city streets.

But relatively few black victims are murdered by whites. Democrats don't need the KKK to kill black people anymore, because black men living on the modern Democratic urban plantation kill each other, mostly over drugs and other crime.

151

A recent news article told of a black father whose nephew was killed in 2003, apparently in a dispute over money. His son was killed in 2007 by a victim he was attempting to rob, and his cousin was killed in 2009 in a dispute over drugs. [lxix]

He is now asking other fathers to pay more attention to their kids, ask them questions, and be more involved in their lives, as he participates in a campaign to reduce the violence.

The Bureau of Justice Statistics (BJS) and National Crime Victimization Survey show that, depending on the number of years included, 91 to 94 percent of the roughly 7,000 black murder victims each year are killed by other black people.

A much smaller percentage of violent crime is interracial, but BJS numbers show that over 80 percent of interracial violent crime today is black-on-white, which is why we don't hear that. The facts don't fit the MMP narrative of dominant white on black crime, which may have been the case while Democrats were terrorizing black people as members of the KKK.

Misguided Outrage and Indignation

The point here is not that whites should feel violent outrage and indignation toward blacks. We don't need any more violent outrage and indignation. But we need to stop letting Democrats use MMP to incite outrage and indignation over falsehoods.

MMP Incites Violence Against Police and Civilized Society

Besides hiding the truth, distorting the facts, and lying to us, MMP treats interactions between citizens and police officers as invitations to fight. When a resisting or attacking suspect is not holding a gun, MMP accuses the cop of brutality if he doesn't run away or wrestle him, as if nothing else would be fair.

But the cop isn't there for a wrestling match to entertain the media. If you fight him or otherwise put him in danger of losing control of his weapon, you endanger his life and yours.

MMP promotes outrage over almost every death of a black person during a struggle with police, but ignores deaths of whites under the same circumstances. Any death of a person during an arrest is bad, but more white lives end that way than black lives.

When a black person points a weapon at a police officer and loses his life as a result, he's called a victim, and the incident is reported a police shooting. MMP portrays almost any white police officer's use of force against a black person as racist misconduct or a crime, and demands "justice."

Police Protect Black and White Lives and Freedom

Police are necessary to maintain freedom and civil order for the benefit of all citizens. People who are constantly subjected to violent crime and chaos are not free. Most police officers do their jobs professionally and properly, saving thousands of black and white lives, while risking their own lives daily.

However, as with any other group of people, there are a few bad police officers who use excessive force or abuse their authority. They should be held accountable for their criminal misconduct and their police powers should be revoked.

Some have taken wrongful actions that have killed innocent people. Their actions are inexcusable and should be prosecuted, but such cases of extreme police misconduct today are rare.

Sacrificing Black Lives for Political Gain

MMP and Democrats including President Obama encourage riots, violent crime, and looting by calling those criminal acts "protests," and the violent criminals "protesters," while both black and white people are hurt and their property is destroyed.

More black lives are endangered if police back down under pressure from MMP and groups such as "Black Lives Matter."

But black lives don't really matter to Democratic leaders, who see dead black men as political opportunities.

If You Vote for Democrats, Do Black Lives Matter to You?

With very few, mostly-local exceptions, votes for Democrats support people to whom black lives are simply ammunition in their battle for power. Black lives have never mattered to Democratic leaders, and they never will as long as Democrats own the votes of black Americans.

34

Freedom Lets All Lives Matter

Free and Successful Black Americans

Many black Americans are famous and highly successful. Some whom I admire are economics professor and author Walter E. Williams, Supreme Court Justice Clarence Thomas, former Secretary of State Condoleezza Rice, economist Thomas Sowell, and brain surgeon Dr. Ben Carson.

Many black men and women who are among my friends and acquaintances are also successful in their jobs and their lives, although not famous.

They include business owners and entrepreneurs, sales professionals, a package delivery service provider, a college math professor, police officers and firefighters, a software developer, a police sergeant, a fire captain, factory workers, a district fire chief, an engineer, a collections agent, teachers, business supervisors, managers and a director, city councilmen, fitness trainers, a Certified Public Accountant, coaches, a high school principal, a computer systems consultant, a security agent, and others. Quite a few are military veterans.

Although not famous, these black Americans are achieving success through their own hard work, perseverance, intelligence, and other capabilities. They have different goals and desires and their own ways of doing things. But they generally have a few things in common.

They do what it takes to achieve their goals in their work. They respect themselves, their wives, husbands, and children, and other people. They value education, hard work, and their families and friends. Many of their lives are devoted to raising their children and making a better future for them. In other words, they are much like the successful white Americans among my friends and acquaintances.

They make their own success, working hard for everything they have, but some don't recognize that Republicans have made their success possible by protecting their natural rights.

Freedom Enabled Their Success

Republicans never claimed to love black people or be their champions. They never claimed that blacks are an inferior race, or promised to control and take care of them, as Democrat slave owners claimed to do, and as Democrats still claim to do today.

That's because Republicans never believed it. They simply recognized that black people were human beings who possessed natural rights, too, while Democrats treated them as property.

Republicans abolished slavery and established the full citizenship and voting rights of the former slaves and their descendants, fighting Democrats every step of the way.

While Democrats rode as the KKK, terrorizing and lynching black men, Republicans proposed civil rights and anti-lynching laws that Democrats defeated. Republicans finally succeeded with the Civil Rights Acts of 1957 and 1960, against strong resistance by Democrats, led by Lyndon B. Johnson.

Republicans cast the deciding Senate votes to defeat a Democratic filibuster against the 1964 Civil Rights Act.

Republicans continue to oppose treating black Americans as an inferior race who need to be controlled, fed, and taken care of. Instead, they promote equal treatment and equal education.

Yet some of my black friends who are free and successful men and women, and millions of whites who say they care about freedom and equal rights, still believe the fairy tale drilled into us for over 50 years that Democrats are "helping" black people.

Martin Luther King's Dream

We have all the rights MLK fought for, but will never live his dream until we demand equal protection, take responsibility for ourselves, and work together.

Black Americans can vote now, and are certainly capable of showing State identification cards or anything else required of white citizens to vote. MMP wants us to believe black people aren't capable of something so simple because the requirement makes it harder for illegal aliens to vote for Democrats.

Undoing the Damage to Protect Our Freedom

Education is the key to undoing the damage. Schools must demand excellence from students regardless of race, and quit passing black students through with fraudulent diplomas.

We must demand equal educational opportunity, including the use of vouchers to achieve it. Parents must take a strong role whether their children are in public or private schools.

We must strive for and celebrate achievement, not diversity. Democrats push diversity to keep black people segregated on urban plantations, under their control. It's OK to be different, but successful people of all races focus on achievement.

Two Strong Black Voices for Freedom

Dr. Ben Carson, during his campaign for the Republican presidential nomination, wrote in a 2015 USA Today article,

"The "BlackLivesMatter" movement is focused on the wrong targets, to the detriment of blacks who would like to see real change and to the benefit of its powerful white liberal funders..."

"The notion that some lives might matter less than others is meant to enrage. That anger is distracting us from what matters most. We're right to be angry, but we have to stay smart.

"Of course, the protesters are right that racial policing issues exist and some rotten policemen took actions that killed innocent people. Those actions were inexcusable and they should be prosecuted to deter such acts in the future.

"But unjust treatment from police did not fill our inner cities with people who face growing hopelessness. Young men and women can't find jobs. Parents don't have the skills to compete in a modern job market. Far too many families are torn and tattered by self-inflicted wounds. Violence often walks alongside people who have given up hope..."

"Let's tell them, we don't want to be clothed, fed and housed. We want honor and dignity." [lxx]

Milwaukee County Sheriff David A. Clarke Jr., a long-time Democrat, wrote in a 2016 Fox News article,

"Democrats are continuing their fifty-year assault on the Black community, adding to it this season with the normalization of criminal behavior and demonization of law enforcement..."

"The Democrat Party's embrace of chaos and criminality is the last step in breaking the backs of this community...the left has pursued policies that keep the Black community dependent, destitute, and demoralized – and fed them crumbs to assure their loyalty..."

"By the time this party is through ensuring each and every poor Black man and woman raises their children on the Democrat plantation of welfare, dependency, and animosity toward their neighbor, there will be many more grieving mothers and fathers..."

"The party that congratulates itself for representing Black America has used them all, destroying them as they seek to grow the might and power of the government and destroy the family, the church, and the American spirit of unity. Through the marginalization of Black fathers...the progressive left has cut off one of the lifelines to raising healthy, happy, children intent on bettering themselves and their community..."

"The men and women I work with in law enforcement deal with the consequences of the Democrats' selfish policies to encourage reliance on government, dependency instead of independence, and victimhood instead of the promise of earning your way to financial security. By the time we interact...the police are met with aggressive and often dangerous challenges to our attempt to keep the peace and protect the community..."

"The Democratic Party is asking Americans to stomach one more divide: the divide from our belief, our hope, our faith that the law can be the great equalizer, protector, and symbol of self-rule. They are asking us to agree with the Democratic Party that the only element worth holding up from our Black communities

157

is the disregard for law and order, and the grief and destruction of families that goes along with it..."

"It's time for Black America to divide itself from this party we've been falsely connecting ourselves to for fifty years and return home to the party of Frederick Douglass, the party of emancipation, the party of equality under the law and equal opportunity for all." [lxxi]

A Few of Many Black Voices for Freedom

Nothing against white voices, but a growing number of other prominent black voices advocate freedom, including:

Walter E. Williams, Economist, College Professor, Author, Newspaper Columnist, occasional Radio Host

Thomas Sowell, Economist, College Professor, and Author

KCarl Smith, Author of *Frederick Douglass Republicans,* Speaker, and Activist: www.frederickdouglassrepublican.org

Ben Carson, Retired Neurosurgeon, Author, and Educator

Clarence Thomas, US Supreme Court Justice, Author

Allen B. West, Former US Congressman, Author, Political Activist, Retired US Army Officer

Frances Rice, Chairwoman of the National Black Republican Association, Retired US Army Officer: www.blackrepublican.blogspot.com

Frantz Kebreau, Author of *Stolen History,* Speaker, Activist

Alan McIntyre, Frederick Douglass Republicans; America Speaks Out, Black on Black Commentary: www.theflypod.com

Condoleezza Rice, Former US Secretary of State, Author

David Clarke, Sheriff of Milwaukee, www.sheriffclarke.com

J.C. Watts, Former Congressman and Business Leader

J. Kenneth Blackwell, Former Ohio Secretary of State

C. L. Bryant, Radio Talk Show Host

35

Freedom for All or Freedom for None

The Country of Freedom for All

When people truly live together in freedom, each person's freedom is limited by the right of others to be free, but no more than necessary for that purpose.

Transformed to Freedom for None

The fight by Democrats to subjugate other people through slavery, segregation, and socialism is not just a conflict over a political preference, but direct opposition to the basic principle that all human beings possess God-given natural rights, and to the limited government our founders built to protect our rights.

We are losing our freedom, security, peace, and prosperity because they are winning, and they have all but extinguished the US Constitution's ability to protect our rights and freedom.

They have almost completed the fundamental transformation to complete socialist control that President Obama promised us.

Freedom vs. Slavery, Segregation, and Socialism

Democratic leaders tell us they know what's best for us, and anyone who opposes them is just squabbling over details.

But the purpose of a government of free people is to protect our rights to life, liberty, and enjoyment of life, not to force others to feed, clothe, house us, and pay our medical bills.

It's easy to see how slavery and segregation deny the natural rights of their victims, but not as easy to see how socialism does, because socialists keep promising to give us anything we want.

The catch is that socialism denies human rights in favor of government rights. It is impossible to live in a free country and at the same time force others to pay for everything we need or want. We can see that clearly when we look at what the years of Democratic socialism have done to all of us.

Final Extinction of Freedom is in Progress

Our national debt is $19 trillion and rising. On the brink of economic disaster, our government is stealing from our children and grandchildren by borrowing more, effectively enslaving them to pay for destroying our freedom and theirs.

Millions of Americans depend on a bankrupt Social Security System with no fund to pay benefits, and no legal obligation to pay. Every payment depends on tax collections and borrowing.

Millions more depend on food stamps and welfare payments from the same bankrupt federal government.

Our president and his chosen successor encourage violent criminals to cross our borders, enable them to kill Americans, and enable terrorist attacks on us within our borders.

They enable Muslim terrorists to obtain nuclear bombs and other weapons to kill us, and promote their "peaceful intentions" in our schools. Mosques, which also serve as forts elsewhere, are strategically located in our cities and along our highways.

Our national defense under Democrats will be incapable of standing up to Russia, China, North Korea, Iran, or ISIS.

Alan McIntyre, of the Frederick Douglass Republicans and the Low Information Voter Project wrote,

"Americans pay tens of thousands of dollars to educate their children, only to have them indoctrinated into accepting a world view that portrays America as an oppressive force that must be stopped. Today's America consists of young black kids supporting the fraudulent Black Lives Matter movement, young white girls believing conservatives are waging a war on women, young black girls murdering their babies at Holocaust proportions, and black men killing themselves through violence and drug abuse, on Democrat controlled, urban plantations." [lxxii]

The Problems with Republicans

When Republicans held the power to make a major change, they used it to abolish slavery. Only Democrats have held that much power during the last 80 years, and have continuously used it to destroy the rights of black Americans and all Americans.

Republicans now hold thin majorities in both Houses, but cannot override a veto, so they back down to the president, the Democratic Minority, the federal bureaucracy, and MMP.

Whenever Republicans try to stop Congress from making all of us pay for even one repressive federal program, the president and Democrats threaten to shut down the federal government and waste even more of the trillions of dollars they're stealing from our children and grandchildren.

The federal bureaucracy is set up so that most employees get paid anyway, so the main losers in a shutdown are the taxpayers.

MMP persuades Americans that Republicans are the ones threatening the shutdown, and with so many people dependent on government, Republicans submit to the pressure.

Some Republicans compromise too much, and some make mistakes. But with a strong majority, they would be able to stop Democrats from extinguishing our freedom.

We Can Still Restore Freedom

We the People can still preserve our freedom and rights, but if we don't do it now, we will probably lose that ability forever.

American men and women of all ages and races must know more about the history of our country, understand the difference between freedom and socialism, and choose to live in freedom.

A large majority of Americans must vote to remove the force against freedom from power, and keep those we elect focused on equally protecting the freedom and rights of all Americans.

Many Americans are working now to preserve our freedom.

Tea Party Groups, Liberty Coalitions, and Liberty Alliances

Local Tea Party groups, Liberty Coalitions, and Liberty Alliances have risen during recent years among Americans who want to preserve our freedom. They welcome women and men of all ages, races, and many religions as members.

The Tea Party is not a political party, but a loose coalition of freedom advocates who support three basic principles: Limited Government, Fiscal Responsibility, and Free Markets.

Frederick Douglass Republicans

Frederick Douglass taught himself to read and write, escaped slavery, taught others to read and write, and achieved success as a newspaper publisher. He was the face of the Abolitionist Movement, instrumental in founding and leading the Republican Party, a strong advocate of women's rights, an advisor to five Republican Presidents, and a successful capitalist.

Frederick Douglass Republicans are not about race, but about the values of Frederick Douglass: Respect for the Constitution, Respect for Life, Limited Government to protect the freedom of citizens, and Personal Responsibility. A person of any race can be a Frederick Douglass Republican.

Other Freedom Organizations

The Heritage Foundation, Americans for Prosperity, Act for America, Freedom Works, the Media Research Center, National Rifle Association, and other independent organizations are working to defend the freedom of all US citizens.

The Republican Party

The Republican Party is the only organization strong enough to help us restore protection of our freedom now. Even with its problems, it remains the strongest national force for freedom.

Republicans who have given up on winning the votes of black Americans must refocus. Your party was founded to free black slaves from their Democrat masters. You need help from black people now to free us all from subjugation by Democrats.

We the People need to start repairing the damage now, and the Republican Party is the vehicle that can get us there in time.

We Have the Power to Preserve or Lose Our Freedom Now

Republicans have chosen a candidate. Ben Carson's intelligence, commitment to freedom, and ability to make good decisions under pressure would make him a good president.

Ted Cruz has demonstrated his commitment to our principles of freedom and limited government, and would be capable of preserving our freedom as president.

But Donald Trump has been chosen. Ironically, he was promoted by MMP because no one thought he could win the nomination, while "reporters" suggested almost daily that he run as a third-party candidate to split Republicans.

Trump was not the first choice of some Republicans, but his success in business, his ability to bring out the best efforts of others, and his refusal to back down to MMP may make him the best choice to stop the destruction of our freedom.

Governor Mike Pence of Indiana, a defender of freedom and limited government, has been chosen to run with Trump, and it appears that he will have strong influence over policy decisions.

We can't allow a third party candidate to split the freedom vote, as Ross Perot did to help elect Bill Clinton in 1992, and Theodore Roosevelt did to elect Woodrow Wilson in 1912.

Although electing him is necessary to stop the destruction of our freedom, this election is not about Trump. It's about our freedom. Every House and Senate seat is of critical importance.

Millions who oppose our rights and freedom will vote. All they need is a president and a few seats in Congress to install one more socialist Supreme Court justice, extinguish our freedom and destroy the future for our children and grandchildren.

Anyone who fails to actively support freedom now will help Democrats destroy the protection of our rights, including self-defense, freedom of religion, freedom of speech and freedom of the press. Without these rights, we probably won't be able to restore our freedom by voting four years from now.

If we allow socialist / Marxist Democrats to put us in the same position as the defenseless Chinese people on Tiananmen Square, it may be impossible to restore our freedom.

Repairing the Damage and Restoring Freedom

We the People must work to restore our freedom with a new President and Congress who will help us. We must demand that our federal government perform its legitimate function of equally protecting our freedom and natural rights.

Removing the Democratic force against freedom is only the first step necessary to overcome the massive damage they have done. Much more work and consistent effort will be required.

Many steps will be needed, including steps to undo injustices that Democrats continue to direct against black Americans.

Steps to Undo the Damage and Restore Freedom

Restore the strength of our national defense and stop appeasing terrorists.

Secure our borders, enforce immigration laws, and then reform them.

Cut the size of the federal bureaucracy. Eliminate departments, agencies, and waste in all areas.

Ensure equal education regardless of race, and use vouchers to let parents choose better schools. Promote reading to children.

Solve "income inequality" through equal education.

Stop violent crime with more police patrols, better police training, and better cooperation between police and citizens.

End crony capitalism and corporate welfare to create equal opportunity regardless of race or wealth.

Reduce taxes and regulations that discourage free enterprise, and let business owners create jobs on an equal playing field.

Repeal federal ownership interest in our bodies, and protect its victims with better and less expensive health care options.

Stop government seizures of property without due process.

Require Members of Congress to consider and vote on all laws and regulations enacted. Enact few laws, and repeal many.

Stop ruling by Administrative Law and Executive Orders.

Stop spending more than we collect. Balance the budget.

Appropriate federal funds through individual votes, not omnibus appropriations bills.

Stop the EPA wars on jobs, coal, and prosperity.

Stop funding abortion provider Planned Parenthood.

Restore Constitutional protection of our rights. Impeach and remove Supreme Court Justices who violate their oaths of office.

Eliminate federal debt, then repeal and replace the income tax with a fair tax.

Stop "speech police" censorship in schools and government.

Protect victims of Social Security who have paid the taxes all their lives, and victims currently required to pay into this disaster forever. Work to establish a Constitutional replacement.

The Time for a new American Revolution is Now

We need a new American Revolution to restore our freedom, but we won't need a violent one if we use our votes and work together now to preserve our freedom and restore our rights.

If we take action this year, we can begin to accomplish the revolution we need, nonviolently with our votes. There will never be a better way to do it, if one is even possible later.

We don't need a new US Constitution. We need leaders who respect the one we have and will restore its limits.

A summary of the Constitution is in the Appendix, following this chapter. Most of the organizations mentioned above and the people listed in Chapter 34 have websites to provide information.

For now, we still have the tools we need to restore protection of our freedom and natural rights. We need to use our power to vote now while black lives and all American lives still matter.

Reverend King told us 53 years ago, "Now is the time!" [lxxiii]

But today, the time for freedom is probably now or never.

APPENDIX

The Limited Powers Granted

From the People and States to the Federal Government

Through the US Constitution, the people granted powers to the federal government they were creating. It is important to understand these powers, because no other federal powers legitimately exist, except as granted by Constitutional Amendments. A short summary and notes are below. You can easily obtain a copy of the complete original text from any public library, or online. You may want to have a copy of the Constitution on hand for comparison and more details.

"WE THE PEOPLE of the United States, in order to form a more perfect Union, establish Justice, insure domestic Tranquility, provide for the common defence, promote the general Welfare, and secure the blessings of Liberty to ourselves and our Posterity, do ordain and establish this Constitution of the United States of America." lxxiv

Promoting the general welfare meant by performing the duties of the government being created, which were all for the general welfare of all citizens.

The Constitution specifies the powers and duties of the federal government, and divides them among three branches, of which Congress is the most powerful. Congress has exclusive power to make laws. The President's duty is to execute the laws. He can suggest new laws, and he can require a larger majority of Congress to pass a law if he disagrees. The Supreme Court has the power to judge whether the Constitution and the laws of Congress have been applied correctly.

The limits and the division of powers were both important because the people were granting a new government the power to take actions that could cost them their freedom or their lives.

Enumerating these powers would have been unnecessary and completely superfluous if the intention had been to simply grant unlimited powers to the federal government.

Article I. (1) Creates Congress, and grants Congress exclusive power to make laws. "All legislative Powers herein granted shall be vested in a Congress of the United States, which shall consist of a Senate and a House of Representatives."

Federal laws were intended to be few and limited to the powers and duties established by the Constitution. Congress was required to meet only once each year and the sessions were expected to be short.

Vesting all legislative powers in Congress assured the people and the States that they would not be subject to any federal law not reviewed and approved by their Representatives and Senators, such as the administrative laws written today by bureaucrats in the executive branch.

Establishes rules for the election and replacement of Representatives and Senators, the length of their terms, qualifications, compensation, and procedures for enacting legislation and taxes, including presidential veto power and overriding a veto. Each State has two Senators, elected by their State legislature, and a number of Representatives, based on population, elected by the people. The House has the sole power to impeach, and the Senate to try any impeachment.

To limit the voting power of States allowing slavery, only three fifths of the actual number of people held in slavery in that State could be counted for this purpose for as long as they were enslaved. Direct taxes levied against the States would also be apportioned by this formula. (Amendments to the Constitution later abolished slavery and superseded all rules related to it.)

Enumerates the powers granted to Congress:

To lay and collect only certain types of taxes and duties "to pay the Debts and provide for the common Defence and general Welfare of the United States." General welfare meant to pay for the cost to perform the duties of the government being created, for the general welfare of all citizens.

167

To borrow Money on the credit of the United States;

To regulate Commerce with foreign Nations, and among the States, and with the Indian Tribes, to insure that commerce could take place across State borders without unreasonable restrictions.

To establish uniform rules for immigration and bankruptcy.

To coin Money, regulate its value and of foreign Coin, and fix the standards of Weights and Measures.

To punish counterfeiting, establish post offices and post roads, and grant patents and copyrights;

To establish federal courts, inferior to the Supreme Court;

To punish pirates and others who commit crimes at sea;

To declare War.

To raise an Army and Navy, and make rules to regulate them.

To provide for calling forth (State) Militia to execute the Laws of the Union, suppress Insurrections and repel Invasions; and to provide for organizing, arming, and disciplining the militia, and governing them when they are in the service of the United States.

To exercise exclusive power over the District of Columbia, intentionally different from a State, and exclusive authority over all federal property including Forts, Magazines, Arsenals, dock-Yards, and other needful Buildings.

To make all Laws which shall be necessary and proper for carrying into Execution the foregoing Powers, and all other Powers vested by this Constitution in the Government of the United States.

Article I also places further restrictions on federal powers including no prohibition of the slave trade until 1808, adds further taxing and spending limits, restricts the suspension of Habeas Corpus (no confinement without due process), prohibits ex post facto (after the fact) laws, prohibits certain types of restrictions on interstate commerce, and restricts titles of nobility.

.

It also restricts specific powers of the States that conflict with powers granted herein to the federal government.

Article II. (2) Creates offices of President and Vice President, establishes their qualifications and terms, vests executive power in the President, establishes his compensation, oath of office, and procedure for election and succession.

Establishes the President as the Commander in Chief of U.S. military forces, and

Grants him power to require written opinions of executive department heads, and to grant pardons;

Grants him the "Power, by and with the Advice and Consent of the Senate, to make Treaties, provided two thirds of the Senators present concur..."

Grants him the power, with Advice and Consent of the Senate, to "appoint Ambassadors, other public Ministers and Consuls, Judges of the supreme Court, and all other Officers of the United States, whose Appointments are not herein otherwise provided for, and which shall be established by Law..."

Grants him the "Power to fill up all Vacancies that may happen during the Recess of the Senate, by granting Commissions which shall expire at the End of their next Session."

Requires the President to inform Congress on the State of the Union, and to recommend measures. Grants him the power to convene Congress on extraordinary Occasions and at times adjourn Congress, to receive ambassadors, to see that laws are executed, and to commission officers.

Authorizes Impeachment.

Article III. (3) Creates and vests judicial power in the Supreme Court and inferior courts established by Congress. Sets terms of judges as "during good Behaviour," sets rules by which their compensation can be changed by Congress.

169

Grants the Supreme Court judicial power over "all cases in Law and Equity, arising under this Constitution," and laws made under its authority, but grants no power to change the meaning of its words, remove any limits, or expand the power of the federal government.

Defines the types of cases over which the Supreme Court has jurisdiction, further limited later by the 11th Amendment, defines types of jurisdiction the Court can exercise, and requires trial by jury in the State where a crime was committed.

Defines Treason and limits the punishment for Treason.

Article IV. (4) Establishes relationships between laws of different States and federal laws.

Grants Congress the power to admit new States to the Union and the "Power to dispose of and make all needful Rules and Regulations respecting Territory or other Property belonging to the United States..."

Establishes the duty of the United States to "guarantee to every State in this Union a Republican Form of Government," and protect each against invasion, and against domestic violence, upon State request.

Article V. (5) Establishes Amendment procedures, which require a two thirds majority of both Houses of Congress and ratification by three fourths of the States.

Article VI. (6) Assumes national public debt, specifically to pay back Revolutionary War debt, Adopts this Constitution, and laws and treaties made under its authority as the supreme law of the land, by which judges of every State shall be bound. Requires that Senators and Representatives, State Legislators, and all judicial and executive officers, both federal and of the States, shall be bound by Oath or Affirmation to support this Constitution.

Article VII. (7) Establishes ratification procedures, requiring ratification by nine States.

Ratification and the Bill of Rights

Eleven of the thirteen States ratified the Constitution by the end of 1788, some of them demanding amendments to further guarantee that the new federal government would not infringe upon their rights by exceeding the limited powers they granted.

The United States federal government began operating in 1789. The twelfth and thirteenth states ratified the Constitution by 1790.

Amendments demanded by the States followed shortly thereafter. Collectively known as the Bill of Rights, the first ten amendments were ratified together and added to the Constitution in 1791. The U.S. Declaration of Independence and the U.S. Constitution are often called our country's founding documents.

Amendments to the US Constitution

Amendments I through **X** (1-10) Known as the Bill of Rights: see Chapter 8

Amendment XI (11) Limited jurisdiction of the Supreme Court

Amendment XII (12) Changed Presidential election procedure.

Amendment XIII (13) Freed all slaves; abolished slavery: see Chapter 13

Amendment XIV (14) Granted full citizenship to former slaves: see Chapter 13

Amendment XV (15) Established voting rights of former slaves: see Chapter 13

Amendment XVI (16) Granted Congress authority to tax individual incomes. See Chapter 16

Amendment XVII (17) Changed the procedure for electing Senators. See Chapter 16

Amendment XVIII (18) Prohibition; later repealed by the 21st Amendment. See Chapter 16

Amendment XIX (19) Extended the right to vote to women. See Chapter 16

Amendment XX (20) Changed dates of presidential terms and rules of succession.

Amendment XXI (21) Repealed the 18th Amendment.

Amendment XXII (22) Limited number of terms of a President.

Amendment XXIII (23) Granted presidential electors to the District of Columbia.

Amendment XXIV (24) Abolished poll taxes.

Amendment XXV (25) New rules of presidential succession.

Amendment XXVI (26) Fixed the voting age at 18 in all States.

Amendment XXVII (27) Delayed pay raises for Congress.

End Notes

[i] Chelsea Scism, What's life really like in North Korea? One woman's story, 7/28/15

[ii] North Korea warns of new famine as Kim's weight, belligerence balloon, FoxNews.com, March, 2016

[iii] Kim Holmes, The Left Is Embracing Orwellian Policies to Go After 'Climate Deniers' 3/14/2016

[iv] The Constitution of the United States, Ratified 1788

[v] Thomas Jefferson, 1776, Rough Draft of the Declaration of Independence

[vi] Frank Johnson Goodnow, *The American Conception of Liberty and Government*, 1916.

[vii] Marx and Engels, 1848, The Manifesto of the Communist Party and Draft of a Communist Confession of Faith

[viii] Martin Luther King, Jr., *I Have a Dream*, speech, 8/28/1963

[ix] Walter E. Williams, Educational Fraud, November 14, 2014

[x] Thomas Paine, 1776, *Common Sense*

[xi] KCarl Smith, *Frederick Douglass Republicans*, 2011, www.FrederickDouglassRepublican.com

[xii] Thomas Paine, *Common Sense*, 1776

[xiii] The United States Declaration of Independence, 1776

[xiv] The United States Declaration of Independence, 1776

[xv] James Madison, The Federalist Papers, No. 45,

[xvi] The First Ten Amendments to the Constitution of the United States, ratified 1791, all quotes in this Chapter

[xvii] Frederic Bastiat, *The Law*, 1848

[xviii] Frederick Douglass, *Life and Times of Frederick Douglass*, 1892

[xix] Frederick Douglass, *Life and Times of Frederick Douglass*, 1892

[xx] John R. Lynch, *The Facts of Reconstruction*, 1913

[xxi] Frank Johnson Goodnow, *The American Conception of Liberty and Government*, 1916.

[xxii] Karl Marx and Friedrich Engels, *Manifesto of the Communist Party*, 1848

[xxiii] Friedrich Engels, *The Draft of a Communist Confession of Faith*, 1847

[xxiv] Frederic Bastiat, *The Law*, 1848

xxv Amity Shlaes, *Coolidge*, 2013

xxvi Coolidge, Calvin, *Foundations of the Republic: Speeches and Addresses*, 1926

xxvii Lawrence W. Reed, Great Myths of the Great Depression, 1981, 2010

xxviii Thomas Sowell, Another Great Depression? 2008

xxix Lawrence W. Reed, Great Myths of the Great Depression, 1981, 2010

xxx Jim Powell, *FDR's Folly*, 2004

xxxi Martin Tolchin, How Johnson Won Election He'd Lost, New York Times, 2/11/1990

xxxii Desegregation before Brown: Barry Goldwater and the forgotten campaign in Phoenix, National Review Online, April 29, 2013, Kevin D. Williamson

xxxiii Senator 'did homework' on Indian Issues, the Phoenix Gazette, Dec. 3, 1986, Michelle Bearden-Mason and Mike McCloy

xxxiv Barry M. Goldwater: The Most Consequential Loser in American Politics, The Heritage Foundation, 7/3/2014, Lee Edwards

xxxv Barry M. Goldwater: The Most Consequential Loser in American Politics, The Heritage Foundation, 7/3/2014, Lee Edwards

xxxvi Desegregation before Brown: Barry Goldwater and the forgotten campaign in Phoenix, National Review Online, April 29, 2013 | Kevin D. Williamson

xxxvii Frederick Douglass, What The Black Man Wants, 1865

xxxviii Stephen Moore, Unraveling the Poverty Myths Obama is Promoting, The Daily Signal, 5/18/2015

xxxix Thomas Sowell, Liberalism versus Blacks, Creators.com, 2013

xl Frantz Kebreau, Stolen History.com, https://www.youtube.com/watch?v=5NDZ4DG-DmE

xli Frederick Douglass, *Life and Times of Frederick Douglass,* 1892

xlii John R. Lynch, *The Facts of Reconstruction*, 1913

xliii Martin Tolchin, How Johnson Won Election He'd Lost, New York Times, 2/11/1990

xliv Frantz Kebreau, Stolen History.com, https://www.youtube.com/watch?v=5NDZ4DG-DmE

xlv Lee Edwards, 4 Liberal Myths About Ronald Reagan Debunked, June 07, 2015

xlvi Walter E. Williams, Social Security Lies, 5/24/2000

xlvii Michael Batasch, Nobel Prize-winning scientist says Obama is 'dead wrong' on global warming, The Daily Caller, 2015

xlviii Walter E. Williams, Climate Change Really a Ruse for Socialist Agenda, 3/15/2015

xlix Doug G, Ware, Earth heading for a mini-ice age in just 15 years, scientists say, UPI 7/12/2015

l Christopher Booker, The Fiddling With Temperature Data is the Biggest Science Scandal Ever, The Telegraph, 2/7/2015

li George W. Bush, Iraq Speech from White House on national television, 3/17/03

lii George W. Bush, President Addresses the Nation, 3/17/2003

liii Brigitte Gabriel, Act for America newsletter, 11/5/2015

liv Perry Chiaramonte, Packing Heat in Detroit Motown, Fox News, 8/21/2015

lv Thomas Jefferson, Letter to Albert Gallatin, 1817

lvi Thomas Jefferson, Letter to Charles Hammond, 1821

lvii Frederic Bastiat, The Law, 1848

lviii The Enquirer, 2/23/2016

lix Walter E. Williams, Special Favors Insult, Demean Black People, 7/27/2014

lx Walter E. Williams, Money and Politics Can't Fix Black Education, 12/7/2014

lxi Walter E. Williams, Educational Fraud, 2/14/2014

lxii Walter E. Williams, What Would the Civil Rights Pioneers Think? 8/11/2013

lxiii Thomas Sowell, Racial Quota Punishment, 11/18/2014

lxiv Walter E. Williams, Progressive Agenda Harms Blacks, 8/2013

lxv Thomas Sowell, Will Dunbar Rise Again? Creators.com, 2014

lxvi Hannah Sparling, Parents Push Back Against Magnet School Lottery, Cincinnati Enquirer, 8/24/2015

lxvii Walter E. Williams, Black Leaders Have Spurned Public Schools, 10/13/2013 [lxviii] Walter E. Williams, Misplacing the Blame for Blacks' Problems, 3/9/2014

[lxix] Cameron Knight, Father on a Mission after 3 Family Members Shot Dead, 4/6/2016

[lxx] Ben Carson, USA Today, 9/3/2015

[lxxi] Sheriff David Clarke, Fox News, 7/26/2016, My message for America's black community: It's time to leave the Democratic Party

[lxxii] Alan McIntyre, To Fellow Defenders of Freedom, 2/ 2016

[lxxiii] Martin Luther King, Jr., *I Have a Dream*, speech, 8/28/1963

[lxxiv] The Constitution of the United States, ratified 1789, all quotes in this Appendix

www.ingramcontent.com/pod-product-compliance
Lightning Source LLC
Chambersburg PA
CBHW031318040426
42443CB00005B/119